TWENTY-FIVE YEARS IN THE
BLACK BELT

Twenty-Five Years in the Black Belt

WILLIAM J. EDWARDS

with an Introduction by
Daniel T. Williams
and an Epilogue by
Consuela Lee

The University of Alabama Press
Tuscaloosa and London

Library of Congress Cataloging-in-Publication Data

Edwards, William James, b. 1869.
    Twenty-five years in the Black Belt / William J. Edwards, with an
introduction by Daniel T. Williams and an epilogue by Consuela Lee
    p. cm.—(The Library of Alabama classics)
    Originally published: Boston, Mass. : Cornhill Co., c1918.
    Includes bibliographical references (p.).
    ISBN 0-8173-0716-8 (alk. paper)
    1. Snow Hill Normal and Industrial Institute (Ala.)—History.
I. Title. II. Series.
LC2851.S575E35   1993
378.761'38—dc20   93-19789

British Library Cataloguing-in-Publication Data available

TO MY LOVING WIFE WHO ENCOURAGED ME IN ALL MY
EARLY STRUGGLES AND AIDED ME IN
ALL MY ACHIEVEMENTS

CONTENTS

LIST OF ILLUSTRATIONS viii

INTRODUCTION *by Daniel T. Williams* ix

PREFACE xv

1. CHILDHOOD DAYS 1
2. SHADOWS 7
3. A RAY OF LIGHT 13
4. LIFE AT TUSKEGEE 18
5. RECONNOITERING 26
6. FOUNDING THE SNOW HILL SCHOOL 35
7. SMALL BEGINNINGS 37
8. CAMPAIGNING FOR FUNDS IN THE NORTH 43
9. RESULTS 49
10. ORIGIN OF THE JEANES FUND 54
11. APPRECIATION 56
12. GRADUATES AND EX-STUDENTS.............. 63
13. THE SOLUTION OF THE NEGRO PROBLEM 77
14. THE GREATEST MENACE OF THE SOUTH 86
15. THE NEGRO EXODUS 94
16. THE NEGRO AND THE PUBLIC SCHOOLS
    OF THE SOUTH 100
17. WHERE LIES THE NEGRO'S OPPORTUNITY?.... 104
18. SCHOOL PROBLEMS OF A
    TUSKEGEE GRADUATE.................. 109
19. BENEFITS WROUGHT BY HARDSHIPS 115
20. THE NEGRO AND THE WORLD WAR.......... 120
    APPENDIX 127
    EPILOGUE *by Consuela Lee* 145

LIST OF ILLUSTRATIONS

WILLIAM J. EDWARDS   xiv

UNCLE CHARLES LEE AND HIS HOME IN THE
     BLACK BELT . . . . *Facing Page* 32

FIRST TRUSTEES OF SNOW HILL AND TWO
     OF THEIR WIVES . . . .   "   "   36

PARTIAL VIEW OF SNOW HILL INSTITUTE .   "   "   48

A NEW TYPE OF HOME IN THE BLACK BELT   "   "   52

TYPICAL LOG CABIN IN THE BLACK BELT .   "   "   60

HOME OF A SNOW HILL GRADUATE . . .   "   "   60

GRADUATES OF SNOW HILL INSTITUTE . .   "   "   72

TEACHERS OF SNOW HILL INSTITUTE . .   "   "   100

INTRODUCTION

DANIEL T. WILLIAMS

Twenty-Five Years in the Black Belt is the memoir written by William J. Edwards in 1918 after a quarter century as founder and principal of Snow Hill Institute, a "little Tuskegee" situated in rural Wilcox County, Alabama. The work not only reveals the conditions of blacks and of race relations in Alabama between 1890 and 1917, but it also tells of one person's great determination to uplift his race, particularly through education, in the years following Reconstruction.

Edwards was an outstanding early alumnus of Tuskegee Institute. He was born on September 12, 1869, in the community of Snow Hill, and his childhood was marred by illness, deprivation, and hunger. His mother died before his first birthday, and his father placed William and two other children with their grandmother.

The family lived on three rented acres and raised cotton and corn. Before his grandmother's death in 1880, Edwards had obtained enough schooling to be able to read. His father moved the family to Selma, where he was employed, and Edwards soon developed a crippling illness that affected his bones. An aunt, learning of his condition, moved him back to Snow Hill, where he performed light chores and continued to read the Bible. The illness persisted, and Edwards's aunt sought treatment from Dr. George W. Keyser in Richmond, Alabama, about ten miles distant. "Beginning in 1884, Keyser operated on Edwards several times . . . and visited him for several months until Edwards recovered."[1]

While attending a revival meeting in Snow Hill in 1887, Edwards heard about Tuskegee, where it was possible to work one's way, and about Booker T. Washington. He rented several acres of land, raised some crops, and used the proceeds to enter Tuskegee in 1889. Four years later he graduated second in a class of twenty. Washington had a profound influence on Edwards and instilled in him the virtues of hard work, self-discipline, and self-respect. Seeking to carry these values into life, Edwards began his journey of helping the brother farthest down. The vision of duty to the unfortunate that Washington had placed before him decided Edwards's life work.

Upon his graduation from Tuskegee in 1893, Edwards toured the black belt counties of Wilcox, Monroe, Butler, Dallas, and Lowndes entirely on foot in order to observe the living conditions and the farming practices of blacks. He discovered that the region contained "a colored population of more than 200 thousand and a school population of 85,499; that the people were ignorant and superstitious; that the teachers and preachers for the most part were of the same condition; that there were no public or private libraries and reading-rooms to which they had access; and that, strictly speaking, there were no public schools and only one private one."

Edwards determined to establish a school for the purpose of elevating the black population in Alabama's
black belt counties, and in fall 1893 he founded Snow
Hill Institute. The new school was modeled after
Tuskegee Institute in its emphasis on the practical and
industrial arts.

As he built his school, Edwards also had to contend
with racial tensions and many political and educational inequities in Alabama. Between 1893 and 1915,
120 blacks were lynched in the state, including 3 in
Wilcox County and 19 in contiguous counties. A school
law of 1891 granted local school authorities complete
control over the distribution of state funds to black and
white schools. The results of this law were illustrated
by public school expenditures in Wilcox County. Money
spent in 1889–90 amounted to $1.02 per white and
ninety cents per black student. The per capita expen-
diture for white students reached $27.75 in 1911–12,
while only fifty-four cents went to educate each black
child that year. In addition, the average length of the
public school term was 6.7 months for whites, com-
pared to only 3.9 months for blacks. These inequities
took their toll. By 1910 black illiteracy in Wilcox
County reached 50.4 percent, while only 4.4 percent of
the white residents could not read and write. Blacks
lost not only educational benefits, but also their right
to vote. The new Alabama Constitution of 1901 dis-
enfranchised black people and prevented any political
efforts to protest the inequities in education.

Edwards was the only teacher when the school opened
as The Snow Hill Colored Literary and Industrial Institute, and despite opposition from local black clergy,

who wanted to see the school operated as an A.M.E.
school, Edwards enjoyed the support of Booker T. Washington and a white plantation owner, R. O. Simpson,
who donated the land for the first buildings. Later
Simpson sold half of his plantation to the school,
"making in all nearly two thousand acres." In 1904 the
name was changed to Snow Hill Normal and Industrial
Institute.

By 1907 Snow Hill enrolled between 300 and 400
students, who were taught by 27 teachers. The physical
plant included 16 buildings. Edwards set forth his philosophy of education in the Minutes of the Board of
Trustees on May 1:

We believe that the ultimate end of education for one people should be that
of any people. Our purposes are to influence young men and women to go
into the communities where they propose to work and, by precept and
example, encourage the people to build better school houses and lengthen
the terms; to influence the people to buy land and build dwelling houses
having more than two rooms, and to bring about any needed reform that is
essential to economic and upright living. Our ultimate end is character
building; our books are not ends, but they are means to an end.[2]

In 1921 Snow Hill Institute maintained a faculty of
25 and owned 24 buildings and 1,800 acres of land,
valued at $150,000. Students represented 33 Alabama
counties and 8 other states.

Edwards resigned in 1924 because of ill health, and
he was succeeded as principal by Harry Simms. The
Institute was in debt, but Simms obtained aid from the
Phelps Stokes Fund, and he reestablished agricultural
extension work for black farmers, as well as money
from the Anna T. Jeanes Fund for supervisory work for
the black schools in Wilcox County.

Ligon A. Wilson became principal in 1929 and

served until 1948. Although he inherited debt, eventually he placed the school on a sound financial footing. Snow Hill Institute became a public school in 1936, and it was closed in 1973 as one result of the desegregation of the Wilcox County schools. William J. Edwards died in 1950 at age 81, having achieved his goal of helping rural black people through education.[3]

NOTES

1. Robert G. Sherer, *Subordination or Liberation? The Development and Conflicting Theories of Black Education in Nineteenth Century Alabama* (University: The University of Alabama Press, 1977), 73.

2. Quoted in Joseph Davis, "A Historical Study of Snow Hill Normal and Industrial Institute and Its Contributions to the Educational Program of the State of Alabama." Unpublished master's thesis, Alabama State College, 1954, 20.

3. Davis, 23–25. In addition to the works by Sherer and Davis, critical assessments of Edwards and of Snow Hill are found in *Between Struggle and Hope: Four Black Educators in the South, 1894–1915,* by Arnold Cooper (Ames: The Iowa State University Press, 1989), and *Fallen Prince,* by Donald P. Stone (Snow Hill: The Snow Hill Press, 1990).

WILLIAM J. EDWARDS

PREFACE

In bringing this book before the public, it is my hope that the friends of the Snow Hill School and all who are interested in Negro Education may become more familiar with the problems and difficulties that confront those who labor for the future of a race. I have had to endure endless hardships during these twenty-five years, in order that thousands of poor negro youths might receive an industrial education,—boys and girls who might have gone into that demoralized class that is a disgrace to any people and that these friends may continue their interest in not only Snow Hill but all the schools of the South that are seeking to make better citizens of our people. I also hope that the interest may be sustained until the State and Nation realize that it is profitable to educate the black child as well as the white.

To me, these have been twenty-five years of self denial, of self sacrifice, of deprivation, even of suffering, but when I think of the results, I am still encouraged to go on; when I think of the work that Mr. McDuffie is doing at Laurinburg, N. C., Brown at Richmond, Ala., Knight at Evergreen, Ala., Mitchell at W. Butler, Ala., Carmichael at Perdue Hill, Ala., Brister at Selma, Ala., and hundreds of others, I feel that the sacrifice has not been in vain, so I continue believing that after all the great heart of the American people is on the right side. I think that to-day, the Negro faces the dawn,—not the twilight,—the morning,—not the evening.

In my passionate desire to hasten that time and with the crying needs of my race at heart, I choose this opportunity for making an appeal in their behalf.

"Lord, and what shall this man do?" (John 21.)

Man is a relative being and should be thus considered. The status of my brother then will always serve as a standard of value by which my own conduct can be measured; by his standard mine may become either high or low, broad or narrow, deep or shallow. This is the theory that underlies all humanitarian work. This is the great dynamic force of the Christian life.

No question is being asked by the American people more earnestly today than this one: "Lord, What shall this man, the Negro, do,—this black man upon whom centuries of ignorance have left their marks?" He has made a faithful slave, a courageous soldier, and when trained and educated, an industrious and law-abiding citizen, yet he is troubled on every side. What shall he do? Uneducated, undisciplined, untrained, he is often ferocious or dangerous; he makes a criminal of the lowest type for he is the product of ignorance.

Crime has increased in proportion as educational privileges have been withdrawn. This brings the Negro face to face with a most dangerous criminal force. What shall this man do? It is true that the white man is further up on the ladder of civilization than the Negro, but the Negro desires to climb and has made rapid strides, according to his chances.

Christ's answer to Peter was, "What is that to thee, follow thou Me." John's future welfare evidently depended upon Peter's ability to follow Christ. So the future work and welfare of the Negro in the Black-Belt of the South depend largely upon the Christian work of the southern white man. The Negro needs justice and mercy from the courts of the land and asks for equal rights in educational opportunities.

We admit that there is a difference between the white man and the Negro, but the difference is not as great as was the difference between Christ and His disciples. We admit that the white man is above the Negro, but not so high as was Christ above His disciples. The very fact that Christ was superior to His disciples served to Him as a reason why He should minister unto them. The superiority of the white man to his black brother can only be shown by the white man's willingness to minister unto him. Lord, what shall this black man do?

Many great problems confront the people of the rural South, namely, this Negro Problem and the problem of sufficient labor supply. In a practical way I wish to consider the relation of the Negro to the labor problem of the rural South. It is a fact that today many of the best farms of the South have been turned into pastures because of the lack of labor; other farms have been sold, and still others are growing up in weeds because there is no one to till them. This condition obtains in a very marked degree in almost every southern state. Certainly in most of the Agricultural Sections.

Before investigating the cause of this condition, men

of influence and power have hastened to proclaim through the press and otherwise, that the responsibility rests upon the Negro. They say that the Negro is lazy, worthless, criminal and will not work and therefore they are compelled to have immigrants to work these fields. That there are lazy, worthless and criminal Negroes, we do not deny, but we do deny that as a race they are such.

The facts are these: first, the South, unlike other sections of the country, has not had thousands of immigrants to come into her borders year after year to do her work, but has depended solely upon the increase in her native population for this purpose. This increase has not kept pace with the marvellous growth and development of that section, hence, the cry for labor. Second, scarcity of labor in that section is due in part, to ignorance and a false idea of real freedom. Men with such ideas do not work long in any one place, but rove from section to section and work enough to keep themselves living. This labor is not only unprofitable to the individual, but is not satisfactory to the employers. Third, the labor trouble in the rural South is due mostly to the way in which the landlords and merchants treat their tenants and customers.

The great mass of Negroes in the South either rent the lands or work them on shares. This rent varies according to the kind of crops that are made. If the tenant makes a good crop this year, he must expect to pay more rent the next year, or his farm will be rented to another at higher figures. Of course, the Negroes are ignorant and are unable to keep their own accounts. Sometimes these Negro farmers pay as much as 50%, 75% and 100% on the goods and provisions which they consume during the year.

This method of renting lands and selling goods according to the condition of the crops, is repeated year after year. I know ignorant farmers who have been working under these conditions for twenty-five and thirty years, who have never been able to get more than $15 or $20 in any one year during this period. These are not worthless and shiftless Negroes, but persons who work hard from Monday morning until Saturday night. As a rule, they are on their farms at sunrise, and remain there until sunset. They have their dinners brought to them in the fields. I have seen small families grow into large ones under these conditions. I have also seen infants grow to manhood under same. Now, these people who have been working in this way for twenty-five and thirty years are becoming discouraged. When you ask them why they do not ditch, fertilize, and improve their farms, their answer is, that if they do this, the next year they will either have to pay more rent or hunt another home for themselves.

It seems to be the policy of the landlords and the merchants of the rural South to keep their tenants and customers in debt. It is this abominable method of the landlords and tenants of the rural South more than anything else, that has caused many' of the best farming lands there to be turned into pastures, others to be sold at sheriff sale, and still others to be growing up in weeds. Another menace is loss of fertility of the soil.

The problem is, how can we stop these people from

leaving the country for the cities and other places of public works and again reclaim these waste fields? It was once thought that the places of these Negroes could be supplied by immigrants from foreign countries, but this hope is now almost abandoned. In fact, the few immigrants who have gone into that section have, in many instances, been oppressed almost as much as the Negroes, many have gone to other parts of the country or have returned to their homes. So we find ourselves face to face with large and fertile agricultural areas in the South with no labor to till them.

The remedy of these evils lies in the Negro himself. He is best suited to the work, best adapted to the climate, and understands the southern white man better than anyone else. Furthermore, he knows the white man; knows his disposition and inclinations, and therefore, knows what is so called his place. He feels that justice is wanting in the courts of the South and he therefore tries to avoid all troubles. Most of all, he prays for a chance to work and educate his children. He labors and waits thus patiently because he has faith in the American people. He believes that ere long the righteous indignation of this people will be aroused and like the great wave of prohibition, will sweep this country from center to circumference, and then every man will be awarded according to his several abilities.

These waste places can be reclaimed and the guttered hills made to blossom, only by giving the Negro a common education combined with religious, moral and industrial training and the opportunity to at least own his home, if not the land he cultivates. The Negro must be taught to believe that the farmer can become prosperous and independent; that he can own his home and educate his children in the country. If he can, and he can be taught these things, in less than ten years, every available farm in the rural South will be occupied.

WILLIAM J. EDWARDS.

TWENTY–FIVE YEARS IN THE
BLACK BELT

TWENTY-FIVE YEARS IN THE BLACK BELT

CHAPTER 1.

CHILDHOOD DAYS.

All that I know of my ancestors was told to me by my people. I learned from my grandfather on my mother's side that the family came to Alabama from South Carolina. He told me that his mother was owned by the Wrumphs who lived in South Carolina, but his father belonged to another family. For some cause, the Wrumphs decided to move from South Carolina to Alabama; this caused his mother and father to be separated, as his father remained in South Carolina. The new home was near the village of Snow Hill. This must have been in the Thirties when my grandfather was quite a little child. He had no hope of ever seeing his father again, but his father worked at nights and in that way earned enough money to purchase his freedom from his master. So after four or five years he succeeded in buying his own freedom from his master and started out for Alabama. When he arrived at Snow Hill, he found his family, and Mr. Wrumphs at once hired him as a driver. He remained with his family until his death, which occurred during the war. At his death one of his sons, George, was appointed to take his place as driver.

As I now remember, my grandfather told me that his mother's name was Phoebe and that she lived until the close of the war. My grandfather married a woman by the name of Rachael and she belonged to a family by the name of Sigh. His wife's mother came directly from Africa and spoke the African language. It is said that when she became angry no one could understand what she said. Her owner allowed her to do much as she pleased.

My grandfather had ten children, my mother being the oldest girl. She married my father during the war and, as nearly as I can remember, he told me that it was in 1864. Three children were born to them and I was the youngest; there was a girl and another boy.

I know little of my father's people, excepting that he repeatedly told me that they came from South Carolina. So it is, that while I can trace my ancestry back to my great-grandparents on my mother's side, I can learn nothing beyond my grandparents on my father's side. My grandfather was a local preacher and could read quite well. Just how he obtained this knowledge, I have never been able to learn. He had the confidence and respect of the best white and colored people in the community and sometimes he would journey eight or ten miles to preach. Many times at these meetings there were nearly as many whites as colored people in the audience. He was indeed a grand old man. His name was James and his father's name was Michael. So after freedom he took the name of James Carmichael.

One of the saddest things about slavery was the separation of families. Very often I come across men who tell me that they were sold from Virginia, South Carolina or North Carolina, and that they had large families in those states. Since their emancipation, many of these have returned to their former states in search of their families, and while some have succeeded in finding them, there are those who have not been able to find any trace of their families and have come back again to die.

Sometimes we hear people attempt to apologize for slavery, but slavery at its best was hard and cruel. Often the old slaves tell me of their bitter experience. Even today, there are everywhere in the South many ex-slaves who lived their best days before and during the civil war. Many of these men and women found themselves alone at the close of the war, having been sold away from their families while they were slaves.

I was born at Snow Hill, Wilcox County, Alabama, September 12th, 1869, three-quarters of a mile east of where Snow Hill Institute now stands. My mother died September 9th, 1870, at which time I lacked three days of being one year old. From all I can learn my mother was very religious. She was a great praying woman and almost at every meeting held in the neighborhood she would be called upon to pray. In fact, she was sent for miles around to pray at these meetings. My mother's death left my father with three children, I being the youngest. He succeeded in getting his mother, who was cooking for her white people in Selma, Alabama, to come and take us in charge. My name was Ulyses Grant Edwards, but my grandmother, who had been with white people since emancipation, changed my name to William. I afterward added to this my grandfather's name of James.

My father went away to work and I remained with my grandmother. We lived about one mile from the "quarter,"—that is, the collection of slaves' cabins. We had about three acres of ground cleared around our cabin and my grandmother and I farmed. I do not know how old I was when I began working, for I have been a farm hand ever since I could remember anything. We usually made one bale of cotton each year and about twenty-five or thirty bushels of corn. Sometimes my grandfather would do our plowing and at other times,—as we had no stock,—my grandmother and I worked out for others to get our plowing done.

In the summer time it was the custom for little Negro boys to wear only one garment, a shirt. Sometimes, however, my grandmother would be unable to get one for me and in that case she would take a crocus sack or corn sack and put two holes in it for my arms and one for my head. In putting on a sack shirt for the first time the sensation was extremely irritating. It seemed as if a thousand pins were sticking me all at once, but after a few days it would become all right and I could wear it comfortably. For several summers this was my only garment.

Sometimes we would raise a pig during the summer to kill in the winter and sometimes we had a cow to milk. At such times we had plenty to eat, but at other times we had neither a pig nor a cow and then we had hard times in the way of getting something to eat.

Some days our only diet was corn-bread and corn coffee.

When I was old enough, I was sent to school for two or three months each winter. Here again I had a hard time, as we usually carried our dinner in a little tin bucket. Sometimes I had nothing but bread and when recess came for dinner, I went away by myself and ate my bread and drank water. As long as I could keep out of the way of the other children, no one was the wiser and I did not mind it, but some of the children began to watch me and in that way found that I had nothing but bread, and when they told the others, they would laugh and make fun of me. This would make me feel badly and sometimes I cried, but I did not stop school for this. My one desire was to learn to read the Bible for my old grandmother, who like my mother, was very religious. At last I was able to read the Bible for her. She would listen for hours and too, she would sing such songs as, "Roll, Jordan Roll."

Saturdays were mill days and I had to take the corn on my shoulder and go to the mill, which was four or five miles away. It always took me from four to five hours to make this trip, as I had to stop by the way several times to rest.

By this time my brother and sister were large enough to do good work on the farm. My grandfather and grandmother for whom they were working, now desired to take them wholly from my old grandmother. The Justice of the Peace said that the children might decide the matter. My brother chose to go to my grandfather's but my sister came back home with the grandmother who had reared us from infants. Of course, I did not go to court, because they all knew that there was no chance of my leaving my grandmother.

In the early spring of 1880 while on one of my trips to the mill the thought dawned upon me that my grandmother was very old and must soon die. I cried all the way to the mill and back. I could not see how I would live after she was gone. I did not tell anybody why I was crying. On a June night, she became severely ill and died. All she said to us during her illness was: "Children, I have been waiting for this hour a long time."

After the death of my grandmother, her daughter Marina Rivers, who was herself a widow and well on in years, came to live with us that year. I soon learned to love her as I had my grandmother and never once thought of leaving her for my mother's people. We gathered the crop that fall and when all was over, my father, whom I had not seen for five or six years, came to carry my sister and myself to Selma, where he was staying. The thought of going to the city filled me with joy and the time to go could not come too soon for me.

CHAPTER 2.

SHADOWS.

We arrived in Selma several days before Christmas. Here everything was strange to me, as I had never been in a city before. I did not know any one and it was not long before I was crying to return to Snow Hill. My father gave me to understand then, that Selma was my home now and that I should not be permitted to return to Snow Hill. He said that he was going to put me in school when the New Year came, but when the time came nothing was said about school. He gave us little care and often we were in need of food and clothes.

After spending a few weeks doing nothing, I went out one day to hunt for work and succeeded in getting a job at the compress, where they reduced the size of a bale of cotton by one-half and clipped the tires. My job was to straighten out the bent tires. I got twenty-five cents a day for this. That week I made one dollar and fifty cents. This was the most money I had ever had. I spent almost all of it for provisions and that night my sister cooked a great supper. Finally, my father said that he would save my wages for me, but if he did he has it still, as I never have seen any that he collected.

I had not been in Selma long before I was taken ill. That misfortune changed my whole life. I had no medical attendance and suffered greatly. Sometimes I prayed and sometimes I cried. The news reached Snow Hill that I was sick and not being cared for. As soon as she could, my aunt Rina came to Selma for me and carried me home.

On my return to Snow Hill I was sick and ema- ciated, but few people welcomed me. Many tried to discourage my aunt for bringing me back. They gave me about three months to live. I was glad to be at home again and had the consolation of knowing that should I die I would be buried in the old burying ground.

I was unable at the time to do any work on the farm, so I was put to the task of raising chickens. I took personal interest in the little chicks. I had a name for each one of them. I would follow them around the yard and see them work for their food. When I was weary of this I would go to an old deserted cabin nearby, taking a few old books and the Bible; there unmolested I would spend hours at a time reading the Bible and pondering over the books. One of the books was an old Davies' Practical Arithmetic. Nothing gave me more pleasure than working out new sums for the first time. I kept up this practice until I had read the New Testament through several times and had worked every problem in the arithmetic. In addi- tion to this I would gather up wood and carry it home for the people to cook with.

My aunt and her daughter were very poor and had to work each day for what they could get to eat. It pained me because I could not go out and work for something to eat as I had done in Selma. I never ate

a full meal although my aunt and her daughter insisted upon my doing so; I felt that I had no right to
eat up what they had worked so hard to get, while I
was doing nothing that was worth while. My aunt's
daughter had a son who was one month older than I;
he was well grown for his age and always was the
picture of health. We all lived in a one-room cabin
and there were three beds in it, besides it was the
kitchen and dining-room as well. My aunt and her
daughter wanted me to sleep at nights with their boy,
but he objected, so I would not force myself upon him.
I asked them to give me one or two old quilts and I
would spread these upon the floor of the cabin at night
for my bed. I would get up early and roll them up
and store them away in some dark corner of the cabin
until the next night. I slept in this manner for several years.

After I had been at home for several months and
my condition did not improve, my aunt went about
begging people for nickels and dimes to take me to
the local physician. I think she raised about three
dollars in this way and succeeded in getting a doctor
to treat me, but he gave my aunt to understand that
she had to pay cash for each treatment.

I shall never forget one Sunday when a great many
of the neighbors came to our home, they began telling
my aunt what they would do with me if they were in
her place. At the time I was in the back-yard watching the chicks. Some one said that she should send
me to the poorhouse, others said that she had done so
much for me, it was time that some of my other people
should take me and share in the burden, while others

said that I should be driven away and go wherever I could find shelter. I was so offended at hearing this that I hobbled down the hill and there under a pine tree, which now stands, I prayed for an hour or more for God to let me die. After this prayer I lay down, folded my arms and closed my eyes, to see if my prayer would be answered. After waiting for awhile I finally decided to get up and I felt better then than I had felt for several months. I have made many prayers since then, but never since have I prayed to die.

None of the solicitations and advices from our good friends could change my aunt's attitude towards me. In fact, she was more determined now than ever to care for me. The next year she rented a little patch and worked it as best she could and that fall she cleared a little money. As the local physician had done me no good, she took me to Dr. George Keyser who lived in the town of Richmond, eight or ten miles away. Dr. Keyser had the reputation of being the best physician in that section of the state and people would come for twenty-five and thirty miles around to be treated by him. But we had also heard that he was a man who would not treat any one without having his money down. As I remember, my aunt paid him five dollars on the first visit and each time after that she would send whatever she could get. I used to borrow a mule from one of the neighbors to ride to see him. Sometimes when my medicine gave out and I had to go without any money, I would pray to God the whole distance that he might soften the doctor's heart so that he would let me have my medicine. I don't know whether my prayers were needed or not, but I do know that the doctor always treated me kindly and finally he told me that I could be treated whenever my medicine gave out, money or no money. He treated me in this way until the early fall of '84 when he told my aunt that I needed an operation and she must try and get me a place to stay nearby so that he could see me daily. After looking around she found on the doctor's place an old fellow-servant, that is, an old lady who belonged to the same man my aunt did in slavery time. Her name was Lucy George; she was near the age of my aunt, and had never been married. They were indeed glad to meet and she readily consented to take me to her little cabin where she lived alone. The doctor visited his plantation two or three times a week and usually came to see me. He operated on me twice during my stay there.

"In 1883 the subject of this sketch, W. J. Edwards, was sent to me by his aunt, Rina Rivers, for medical treatment. He had been sick for several months from scrofula and it had affected the bone of his left arm (hinneras) near the elbow joint, and the heel bone (os calcis) of his left foot. It was with much difficulty and pain that he walked at all.

The boy was kind, courteous and polite to every one, white and colored, and all sympathized with him in his great affliction, and manifested their sympathy in a very substantial way, by sending him many good things to eat. This enabled me to build up his general health.

I had to remove the dead bone (necrosed bone) from his arm and heel many times. He always stood the operation patiently and manifested so great a desire to get well, I kept him near me a long time and patiently watched his case.

After four years' treatment his heel cured up nicely, and he was enabled to walk very well, and the following fall he picked cotton. With prudence, care and close application to cotton picking, he saved money enough to very nearly pay his medical account, and his fare to Booker Washington's School at Tuskegee, Alabama.

The work of this pupil of Booker Washington,—carried on under adverse circumstances,—is worthy of emulation. He has, and is now, doing much good work for his race. He has won the confidence and esteem of all the white and colored citizens of this section of the country. He is a remarkable man, a great benefactor to his race, and it affords me great pleasure to testify as to his history and character. Mr. R. O. Simpson, on whose plantation he lived and who aided him materially,—is one of the Trustees of his Institute."

GEORGE W. KEYSER, M. D.

Richmond, Dallas County, Alabama.

CHAPTER 3.

A RAY OF LIGHT.

For three months after my first operation I could not walk. My aunt would come from Snow Hill once a week to bring my rations and to see how I was getting along. I always cried when she went home.

During my first month's stay on the doctor's place, "Aunt Lucy" George with whom I lived, was at home most of the time, but when the cotton season came on, she had to go to the doctor's field, which was a mile away, to pick cotton. This left me alone for five days in the week. "Aunt Lucy" would get up early and prepare her breakfast, take her lunch to the field with her, and would not return until night. She would also leave me something to eat, and I could crawl about the house and get such other things as I needed.

The first few days that I was alone were the most miserable days of my life. I tried to walk, but fainted once or twice at these attempts, so I had to be contented with crawling. Soon, however, I began crawling about the yard. I found several red ants' nests within about twenty or twenty-five yards of the house, and soon made friends of the ants. I would crawl from nest to nest and watch them do their work. I became so interested in them that I would spend the whole day watching and following them about the yard. I would be anxious for the nights to pass that I might return to them the next day.

I found that the ants worked by classes. One class would bring out the dirt, another would go out in search of food, another would take away the dead, another would over look those that worked, and still another class, though few in numbers, would come out and look around and then return. These had much larger heads than the average. Some few, however, with great heads, would come out once or twice a day. I never learned what their business was, as they did not seem to do much of anything. They very seldom went more than a few inches from the nests. I noticed, too, that those that went in search of food and failed to get it, would come back to the nests and stand around and consult with the guards and then would return. They did this several times. Sometimes they would go away and get into the weeds and rest awhile. However, when they saw others coming, they would start out again. Sometimes, after making several trips without success, I would give them crumbs of bread, and they would hasten away to their nests. They never hesitated when they had food, but would run right in. This was great fun for me, and I spent most of the remainder of my time in this manner.

This was during the fall of '84. By the first week in December I had recovered sufficiently to be able to walk very well with a stick and could do a little work. I then returned to Snow Hill with my aunt, and, though I was anxious to return home, I hated very much to leave my little friends. I got home in time to make toy wagons for my Christmas money.

The following year, although far from being well, I could do a little work on my aunt's farm. I ought not to call it a farm, because it was only a few acres which she rented from one of the tenants on Mr. Simpson's plantation. The habit of sub-renting was very prevalent on this plantation. A tenant with one mule would rent twenty-five acres, if he had two mules he would rent fifty acres. Now in order to get work done on his farm, he would sub-rent four or five acres, to some one who would do this work for him. It was in this way that my aunt could get land to work. We usually made on these few acres about twenty bushels of corn and sometimes a half a bale or a whole bale of cotton.

Having to work for our plowing and to pay the rent of the land, we had but little chance to do much work for ourselves. We very seldom had enough to eat. Some days we would work from the rising of the sun until dark without anything but water. Then my aunt would go out among the neighbors in the evening and borrow a little corn meal or get a little on condition that she would work to pay for it the next day. While my aunt would go to hunt for the bread I would go out and beg for some milk from some of our friends. I would always add water to my milk to make it go a long way. This bread and half-water-and-milk constituted our supper for many nights.

In spite of these hard times I always found time to study my books. Sometimes I borrowed books from the boys and girls who had them. We were too poor to buy oil so I would go to the woods and get a kind of pine that we called light-wood. This would make an excellent light and I could study some nights until twelve o'clock. When the blackberries, peaches, apples and plums were ripe, we fared better, as these grew wild and we could have a plenty of them to eat. As the season came for the corn to mature, we would sometimes make a meal of green corn. When the corn became too hard for us to use in this way, we used to make a grater out of an old piece of tin and would grate the corn and make meal of it in this way until it was hard enough to go to the mill.

When the cotton picking season came on we could pick cotton for the neighbors and in that way could have a plenty to eat. They paid fifty cents a hundred pounds for picking cotton. I sometimes picked two hundred pounds a day, but by picking at night, I occasionally got almost three hundred. We children thought it great fun to go into the swamps at night to pick cotton. We would go at seven o'clock in the evening and spend the whole night in the cotton fields. When we got sleepy we would lie down in the cotton row with our cotton sacks under our heads. We would sleep a few hours and get up and begin picking again. In the swamps at night the owls and frogs made plenty of music for us. Such was my life for several years.

During all these years the one thing uppermost in my mind was the desire to attend some school, but I could not see how I would ever be able to do so. I had heard much of Talladega College, the school at Normal and the state school at Montgomery, but board at these schools was from seven to eight dollars per month and this had to be paid in cash. This, of course, would keep me out, as I could never see how I could get so much money.

It was during the month of August '87 that I first heard of Tuskegee. There was a revival meeting going on at one of the churches at Snow Hill. I was determined to visit this meeting. I did not have suitable clothes, neither did I have any shoes, so my people told me that I would not be able to attend church.

I had not been to church in seven years, and I was very anxious to hear some preaching. Notices were sent out that on a Wednesday night a Presiding Elder would speak. This man had the reputation of being a great preacher. All of our people prepared early, and went to church. When I thought the services had begun, I too went. Though I was far from being well, I did not have much trouble in reaching there. I did not go in, however, but went around to the rear of the church. The building was a large, box-like cottage, and contained many cracks. One could hear as well on the outside as on the inside. I stood directly behind the pulpit and heard all that the preacher said.

At the close of his sermon he spoke of the school at Tuskegee, where, he said, poor boys and girls could go without money and without price, and work for an education. From that night I decided to go to Tuskegee. Before the meeting closed, I returned home, and when the others got there, I was in my place fast asleep. I wrote Mr. Washington the next day, and he sent me a catalogue immediately.

CHAPTER 4.

LIFE AT TUSKEGEE.

In the fall of '87 I told my aunt that I wanted to go to Tuskegee the next year, and that in addition to her little farm, I wanted to rent an acre of land and work it for that purpose. She encouraged me in this idea and said that she wished so much that she could do something for me that was worth while, but she was poor and could do but little, as she was now well advanced in years. She said, however, that she would help me to work my patch.

About this time I learned that my brother Washington, who had been away for a number of years, was living at Hazen, Alabama, about fifty miles northeast of Snow Hill. He was working in the bridge-gang on a railroad and was making good money. I learned also that my father and sister had died several years before. Now as there were but two of us, and I was cripple, I thought that I would write my brother and get him to help me go to Tuskegee. So I started out for Hazen and reached there after two days' journey on foot. My brother did not seem to care for me and gave me no encouragement whatever. This was a sore disappointment to me and I did not remain there more than a few days. I returned to Snow Hill very much discouraged, but the warmth with which my old aunt greeted and welcomed me back home, helped me much.

Soon we were all busy getting ready to plant our little farms. That year there were four of us still living in the one room log cabin, my aunt, her daughter, her grandson and myself. Each of us had a little farm. About mid-summer when our provisions had given out, my aunt's daughter and her son mortgaged their crops for something to eat, and wanted that we should do the same, but I would not agree to do so. This, of course, made it hard for me to get anything to eat. My cousin and her son were perfectly willing that their mother and grandmother should share in their provisions, but would see to it that I got none. I did not think hard of them for this, because I felt that I had no right to what they had. I continued to live on water and bread, and sometimes I would get a little milk from the neighbors as I had formerly done. I asked them, however, if I might have the water in which they boiled their vegetables whenever they had a boiled dinner. We called this water "pot liquor." Of course, they readily consented to this and sometimes I would get enough of this liquor to last me two or three days. In fact, I was poorly nourished all the time.

About this time someone came through the county selling clocks, on condition that we pay for them later in the fall. I objected to this but the other members of the family over-ruled my objections and the clock was bought on the condition stated above. The clock cost $12 and each of us agreed to pay $3.00 each. When the time came to pay for this clock no one had any money, and so I paid what I had saved to prepare myself for Tuskegee. I thought now that I would never get to that school as I had spent most of my money in paying for a worthless clock. However, I picked cotton day and night for almost two weeks, and succeeded in making all the money back which I had spent for the clock. I was now able to finish paying Dr. Keyser and get a few clothes and start for Tuskegee. For a long time the people in the quarter did not believe that I was going, and many tried to discourage me. Had it not been for my aunt's encouraging words and sincere efforts, I believe that I could not have overcome the efforts of others to keep me from going. When, however, they all found that I was determined to go, they all became my friends and each would give me a nickel or a dime to help me off.

The night before I left for Tuskegee, one of the neighbors told me that while he did not have anything to give me, he had a contract to get a cord of wood to the woodyard for the train by six o'clock the next morning and if I would take his team and haul it, he would give me one dollar for my services. I agreed to do it and at two o'clock the next morning I was at his home hitching up the team to haul the wood. I had to go about two miles for the wood and there was a very heavy frost that morning. By five o'clock I had hauled the wood and had the team back to my neighbor's home waiting for my dollar. I thought this to be the coldest morning that I had ever experienced up to that time. I then got my few things together and was off for school.

I reached Tuskegee the first day of '89. I found

things there very strange indeed. Hundreds of students were going to and fro. Some were playing football, others were having band practice, and still others were going around doing nothing, as the first day of the New Year was a holiday. I was placed with a crowd of boys from Pensacola, Fla. I learned afterwards that they were the roughest boys in school. They made it very unpleasant for me, so much so that I decided to return home. In going back to the office I met Mr. Washington for the first time. He wanted to know why I was not satisfied, and after I told him my troubles, he said that he would remedy them. I was deeply impressed with him and from that day to this, I loved him as a father. He changed my room and I found a crowd of very congenial boys.

The next ordeal through which I was to pass, was going into the dining-room and using knives and forks, but I avoided all humiliation by simply watching. I have made it a rule of my life to never be the first to try new things, nor the last to lay old ones aside.

After supper, I was worried about sleeping. I had heard the boys talking about night shirts and I knew I had none; in fact, I did not know their purpose. So when time came to retire, one of the boys in my room who had several, gave me one, then I was undecided just whether it was to go over my day shirt or over my undershirt, but I did not want to ask how it should be worn, so I decided to sit up until some one had gone to bed and by watching him I knew I would learn just how to use mine. In this way I came through all right. The habit of using the tooth-brush was not so hard.

The next day the regular routine work of the school began and I was given my examination. I took examination for the B-Middle class. This is the second year normal. Miss Annie C. Hawley of Portland, Maine, who was then a teacher there, gave me the examination. I made the class in all of the subjects except grammar. Of this subject I knew absolutely nothing. I did not know what a sentence was. I could not tell the subject from the predicate, so I was put back two years into what is called the A-Prep. class.

After my examination I was assigned to my work. I was placed in the tin shop, which was then being placed as one of the industries, under Mr. Lewis Adams. I was the first student to work in this shop, but it did not take two days to learn that I could never be a tinsmith. Next I was assigned to the printing office, but here too I found that I could never become a printer; so finally, I was put on the farm and there I remained during my whole stay at Tuskegee. The farm manager at that time, Mr. C. W. Green, had charge of the brick-yard, poultry, dairy, landscape gardening, horticulture, as well as the general farm and truck-farm. I worked some in all of these departments and enjoyed my work immensely. I considered the work in the brick-yard as being the hardest of all and that was the only work which I could not do without suffering great pain because of my physical condition. Still I was willing to endure suffering if by so doing I could obtain an education.

I did not go to night school because I was given extra work, such as keeping the clocks on the campus regulated and making fires in the girls' buildings, and too, they had a system of electric bells which were used for the passing of classes, and I kept these in order. In this way I worked enough each month to pay my board and stay in day school. Of course, I did not have, or get any money for my work, but I did not worry about that. Miss Maggie Murray (afterwards Mrs. Washington) kept me well supplied with clothes from the supply of second hand garments which came to the school from northern friends.

The remainder of the time that I was at Tuskegee was spent in practically the same way that I have already described. Many of the students would complain about the food, but the fact that I was getting three regular meals a day was enough for me. And too, I was now sleeping in a bed, something that I seldom had done.

When burning bricks they would pay students cash for working at night, and it was by this work that I got a little money now and then. It usually takes from seven to eight days to burn a kiln of brick and sometimes I would work every night until the kiln had been burned.

The one thing that made the deepest impression on me while at Tuskegee was Mr. Washington's Sunday evening talks to the students. He used to tell us that after getting our education we should return to our homes and there help the people. He said that the people were supporting Tuskegee in order that we might be able to help the masses of our people. I could understand every word he said, and too, I felt always that he was talking directly to me. These talks of Dr. Washington's changed the course of my whole life and they are responsible for my being at the Snow Hill School today.

It was when I reached the senior class that I came in personal touch with Dr. Washington, as he taught that class in two or three subjects. Here I could study him as I was never able to do before. He had a thorough grasp upon all subjects he taught and would accept nothing but the same from his students.

As the time was nearing for my graduation, I was deeply worried about my Commencement suit. All of the other members of the class were sending home for their suits or for the money with which to get them, but I knew that my aunt was not able to help me, so I was at a loss to know where I should get mine. Finally, I decided to write to Mr. R. O. Simpson of Furman, Alabama, the man on whose plantation I was reared, and ask him to loan me fifteen dollars. I prayed during the entire time it took me to write the letter and when I had sealed it I prayed over it again. In two days' time I had an answer with the fifteen dollars. So all of my troubles and worries were banished and I proceeded to get ready for Commencement. I graduated second, with a class of twenty, on May 17, 1893. Our class motto was "Deeds Not Words."

The morning of May 18th found me packing my few clothes in an old trunk which one of the young men had given me, and getting ready to return to Snow Hill. All the while I was thinking of what I could do to live up to this new training which I had received at Tuskegee, and above all, how could I make good our class motto: "Deeds Not Words." Although it has been now well nigh 25 years since my graduation, those words still ring in my ears: "Deeds Not Words." I should like so to live that when the summons come for me to join Dr. Washington in the Great Beyond, these words might be written as an epitaph on my tomb:

"DEEDS NOT WORDS."

CHAPTER 5.

RECONNOITERING.

When I returned from Tuskegee on the 19th of May, 1893, I found my old aunt, her daughter and her grandson still living in the one-room log cabin in which I had left them four and a half years before. Their condition was much the same as when I left them. My first work was to build another end, a log pen, to the one room cabin; this gave us two rooms, something we never had before. As it was too late for me to pitch a crop, I worked with them until their crop was clean of weeds and then I went from farm to farm in the neighborhood, helping all the farmers that I could. The only pay I received was three meals a day wherever I worked. I usually worked from one to three days on each farm. All the while I was making a close study of the people's condition. I continued working in this way until I was convinced that I had a thorough knowledge of their condition. I then ventured to carry the investigation into other sections of Wilcox County and the adjoining counties. I visited most of the places in the counties of Monroe, Butler, Dallas and Lowndes. These constitute most of the Black Belt counties of the State. I made the entire journey on foot.

It was a bright beautiful morning in July when I

started from my home, a log cabin. More than two hundred Negroes were in the nearby fields plowing corn, hoeing cotton and singing those beautiful songs often referred to as plantation melodies: "I am going to roll in my Jesus' arms," "O, Freedom," and "Before I'd be a Slave, I'd be carried to my Grave." With the beautiful fields of corn and cotton outstretched before me, and the shimmering brook like a silver thread twining its way through the golden meadows, and then through verdant fields, giving water to thousands of creatures as it passed, I felt that the earth was truly clothed in His beauty and the fulness of His glory.

But I had scarcely gone beyond the limits of the field when I came to a thick undergrowth of pines. Here we saw old pieces of timber and two posts. "This marks the old cotton-gin house," said Uncle Jim, my companion, and then his countenance grew sad; after a sigh, he said: "I have seen many a Negro whipped within an inch of his life at these posts. I have seen them whipped so badly that they had to be carried away in wagons. Many never did recover."

From this our road led first up-hill, then down, and finally through a stretch of woods until we reached Carlowville. This was once the most aristocratic village of the Southern part of Dallas County. Perhaps no one who owned less than a hundred slaves was able to secure a home within its borders. Here still are to be seen stately mansions and among the names of the owners are those of Lyde, Lee, Wrumph, Bibb, Youngblood and Reynolds. Many of these mansions have been partly rebuilt and remodeled to conform to modern styles of architecture, while others have been deserted and are now fast decaying. Usually the original families have sold out or many have died out.

In Carlowville stands the largest white church in Dallas or Wilcox Counties. It has a seating capacity of 1,000, excluding the balcony, which during slavery was used exclusively for the Negroes of the families attending.

Our stay in Carlowville was necessarily short, as the evening sun was low and the nearest place for lodging was two miles ahead. Before reaching this place we came to a large one-room log cabin, 30 by 36 feet on the road-side, with a double door and three holes for windows cut in the sides. There was no chimney nor anything to show that the room could be heated in cold weather. This was the Hopewell Baptist Church. Here five hundred members congregated one Sunday in each month and spent the entire day in eating, shouting, and praising God for His goodness toward the children of men. Here also the three months' school was taught during the winter. A few hundred yards beyond this church brought us to the home of a Deacon Jones. He was living in the house occupied by the overseer of the plantation during slavery. It was customary for Deacon Jones to care for strangers who chanced to come into the community, especially for the preachers and teachers. So here we found rest. At supper Deacon Jones told of the many preachers he had entertained and their fondness for chicken.

After supper I spent some time in trying to find

out the real condition of the people in this section. Mr. Jones told me how for ten years he had been trying to buy some land, and had been kept from it more than once, but that he was still hopeful of getting the right deeds for the land for which he had paid. He also told of many families who had recently moved into this community. These newcomers had made a good start for the year and had promising crops, but they were compelled to mortgage their growing crops in order to get "advances" for the year.

When asked of the schools, he said that there were more than five hundred children of school age in his township, but not more than two hundred of these had attended school the previous winter, and most of these for a period not longer than six weeks. He also said that the people were very indifferent as to the necessity of schoolhouses and churches. Quite a few who cleared a little money the previous year had spent it all in buying whiskey, in gambling, in buying cheap jewelry, and for other useless articles. After spending two hours in such talk, I retired for the evening. Thus ended the first day of my search for first-hand information.

Instead of going farther northward, we turned our course westward for the town of Tilden, which is only eight miles west of Snow Hill. The road from Carlowville to Tilden is somewhat hilly, but a very pleasant one, and for miles the large oak trees formed an almost perfect arch.

On reaching Tilden we learned that there would be a union meeting of two churches that night. I decided that this would give me an opportunity to study the religious life of these people for myself. The members of churches number one and number two assembled at their respective places at eight o'clock. The members of church number two had a short praise service and formed a line of procession to march to church number one. All the women of the congregation had their heads bound in pieces of white cloth, and they sang peculiar songs as they marched. When the members of church number two were within a few hundred yards of the church number one, the singing then alternated, and finally, when the members of church number two came to church number one, they marched around this church three times before entering it.

After entering the church, six sermons were preached to the two congregations by six different ministers, and at least three of these could not read a word in the Bible. Each minister occupied at least one hour. Their texts were as often taken from Webster's blue-back speller as from the Bible, and sometimes this would be held upside down. It was about two o'clock in the morning when the services were concluded. Here, again, we found no schoolhouses, and the three months' school had been taught in one of the little churches.

The next day we started for Camden, a distance of sixteen miles. This section between Tilden and Camden is perhaps the most fertile section of land in the State of Alabama. Taking a southwest course from Tilden, I crossed into Wilcox County again, where I saw acres of corn and miles of cotton, all being cultivated by Negroes.

The evening was far advanced when we reached Camden, but having been there before, we had no difficulty in securing lodging. Camden is the seat of Wilcox County, and has a population of about three thousand. The most costly buildings of the town were the courthouse and jail, and these occupied the most conspicuous places. Here great crowds of Negroes would gather on Saturdays to spend their earnings of the week for a fine breakfast or dinner on the following Sunday, or for useless trivialities.

On Saturday evenings, on the roads leading to and from Camden, as from other towns, could be seen groups of Negroes gambling here and there, and buying and selling whiskey. As the county had voted against licensing whiskey-selling, this was a violation of the law, and often the commission merchant, a Negro, was imprisoned for the offense, while those who supplied him went free.

In Camden I found one Negro school-house; this was a box-like cottage, 20 by 16 feet, and was supposed to seat more than one hundred students. This school, like those taught in the churches, was opened only three months in the year.

After a two days' stay in Camden, I next visited Miller's Ferry on the Alabama River, twelve miles west of Camden. The road from Camden is one of the best roads in the State, and for miles and miles one could see nothing but cotton and corn.

At Miller's Ferry a Negro school-house of ample proportions had been built on Judge Henderson's plantation. Here the school ran several months in the year, and the colored people in the community were prosperous and showed a remarkable degree of intelligence. Their church was as attractive as their school-house.

Judge Henderson was for twelve years Probate Judge of Wilcox County. He proved to be one of the best judges this county has ever had, and even unto this day he is admired by all, both white and black, rich and poor, for his honesty, integrity, and high sense of justice.

From Judge Henderson's place we traveled southward to Rockwest, a distance of more than fifteen miles. During this journey hundreds of Negroes were seen at work in the corn and cotton fields. These people were almost wholly ignorant, as they had neither schools nor teachers, and their ministers were almost wholly illiterate. At Rockwest I found a very intelligent colored man, Mr. Darrington, who had attended school at Selma for a few years. He owned his home and ran a small grocery. He told of the hardships with which he had to contend in building up his business, and of the almost hopeless condition of the Negroes about there. He said that they usually made money each year, but that they did not know how to keep it. The merchants would induce them to buy buggies, machines, clocks, etc., but would never encourage them to buy homes. We were very much pleased with the reception which Mr. Darrington gave us, and felt very much like putting into practice our State motto, "Here We Rest," at his home, but our objective point for the day was Fatama, sixteen miles away.

On our journey that afternoon we saw hundreds of

UNCLE CHARLES LEE AND HIS HOME IN THE BLACK BELT

Negro one-room log cabins. Some of these were located in the dense swamps and some on the hills, while others were miles away from the public road. Most of these people had never seen a locomotive.

We reached Fatama about seven o'clock that night, and here for the first time we were compelled to divide our crowd in order to get a night's lodging. Each of us had to spend the night in a one-room cabin. It was my privilege to spend the night with Uncle Jake, a jovial old man, a local celebrity. After telling him of our weary journey, he immediately made preparation for me to retire. This was done by cutting off my bed from the remainder of the cabin by hanging up a sheet on a screen. While somewhat inconvenient, my rest that night was pleasant, and the next morning found me very much refreshed and ready for another day's journey. Our company assembled at Uncle Jake's for breakfast, after which we started for Pineapple.

We found the condition of the Negroes between Fatama and Pineapple much the same as that of those we had seen the previous day. No school-house was to be seen, but occasionally we would see a church at the cross-roads. We reached Pineapple late in the afternoon.

From Pineapple we went to Greenville, and from Greenville to Fort Deposit, and from Fort Deposit we returned to Snow Hill, after having traveled a distance of 157 miles and visiting four counties.

In three of these counties there was a colored population of 42,810 between the ages of five and twenty years, and a white population of 7,608 of the same ages. The Negro school population of Wilcox and the seven adjoining counties was 11,623. Speaking of public schools in the sense that educators use the term, the colored people in this section had none. Of course, there were so-called public schools here and there, running from three to five months in the year and paying the teachers from $7.50 to $18 per month.

Our trip through this section revealed the following facts: (1) That while many opportunities were denied our people, they abused many privileges; (2) that there was a colored population, in this section visited, of more than 200,000 and a school population of 85,499; (3) that the people were ignorant and superstitious; (4) that the teachers and preachers for the most part, were of the same condition; (5) that there were no public or private libraries and reading-rooms to which they had access; (6) that, strictly speaking, there were no public schools and only one private one. Now, what can be expected of any people in such a condition? Can the blind lead the blind? They could not in the days of old, and it is not likely that they can now.

CHAPTER 6.

FOUNDING THE SNOW HILL SCHOOL.

After this trip through the "Black Belt" I was more convinced than ever before of the great need of an Industrial School in the very midst of these people; a school that would correct the erroneous ideas the people held of education; a school that would put most stress upon the things which the people were most likely to have to do with through life; a school that would endeavor to make education practical rather than theoretical; a school that would train men and women to be good workers, good leaders, good husbands, good wives, and finally train them to be fit citizens of the State and proper subjects for the Kingdom of God.

With this idea the Snow Hill Normal and Industrial Institute was started twenty-five years ago in an old dilapidated one-room log cabin with one teacher and three students, with no State appropriation, and without any church or society responsible for one dollar of its expenses. Aside from this unfortunate state of affairs, the condition of the people was miserable. This was due partly to poor crops and partly to bad management on their part.

In many instances the tenants were not only unable to pay their debts, but were also unable to pay their rents. In a few cases the landlords had to provide at their own expense provisions for their tenants. This was simply another way of establishing soup-houses on the plantations. The idea of buying land was foreign to all of them, and there were not more than twenty acres of land owned by the colored people in this whole neighborhood. The churches and schools were practically closed, while crime and immorality were rampant. The carrying of men and women to the chain-gang was a frequent occurrence. These people believed that the end of education was to free their children from manual labor.

They were much opposed to industrial education. When the school was started, many of the parents came to school and forbade our "working" their children, stating as their objection that their children had been working all their lives and that they did not mean to send them to school to learn to work. Not only did they forbid our having their children work, but many took their children out of school rather than allow them to do so. A good deal of this opposition was kept up by illiterate preachers and incompetent teachers, who had not had any particular training for their profession. In fact, ninety-eight per cent of them had attended no school. We continued, however, to keep the "Industrial Plank" in our platform, and year after year some industry was added until we now have fourteen industries in constant operation. Agriculture is the foremost and basic industry of the institution. We do this because we are in a farming section and ninety-five per cent of the people depend upon agriculture for a livelihood.

FIRST TRUSTEES OF SNOW HILL AND TWO OF THEIR WIVES

CHAPTER 7.

SMALL BEGINNINGS.

The early years of the school were indeed trying ones. There are however in all communities persons whose hearts are in the right place. I found it so in this case, for while there were many who opposed the industrial idea, there were those who stood for it and held up our arms. I refer to that noble class of old colored men who always seek for truth. The men who stood so loyally by me in the founding of the school were Messrs. Frank Warren, Willis McCants, Ellis Johnson, John Thomas, Isaac Johnson, Tom Johnson and P. J. Gaines. These men and their wives were ready at every call. They gave suppers, fairs and picnics as well as other entertainments to raise money for the school. Not only would they help in the raising of money, but they would come to the school and work for days without thinking of any pay for their work. When we got ready to put up a new building, we would have what we called a house-raising and would invite all the men in the neighborhood to come out and help us. On these days the wives of these men would compete with each other to see who could bring out the best basket.

At the end of the first school year it was clearly seen that we needed two assistant teachers; but the question that puzzled us was, where could they work. We had only one room and none of us had the money to buy the lumber needed. But there was a saw-mill near by and finally I sought work at this mill with the understanding that I would take my pay in lumber if the people would agree to feed me. This they readily consented to do. So I worked during May, June, July and August at the saw-mill and took my wages in lumber. This enabled us to get sufficient material to erect two of the rooms of our present Training Building. The following October we opened school with three teachers and 150 students. These two teachers had graduated at Tuskegee with me in '93. They were Misses Ophelia Clopton and Rosa Bradford. They spent four years in the work here and we never had two teachers who did more for the old people in the community and who were loved more by them.

In the fall of '95 Mr. Barnes, who was also a member of the class of '93, joined us, and has been connected with the school since then except for two years which he spent in Boston.

In the fall of '96 another one of our class-mates, Julius Webster, a carpenter, joined in our work here. We now had five teachers, all of Tuskegee and all class-mates. I can never forget these old people and these early teachers, for we all shared our many sorrows and our few joys. No work was too hard for us and no sacrifice was too great.

Another Tuskegee student was with us almost from the beginning. While Mr. Rivers did not graduate from the Academic Department at Tuskegee, he finished his trade, Agriculture, there. Mr. Rivers has had charge of our farm off and on since '95. I should say to his credit that he is in charge today and last year he made the best crop the school has ever made.

Thus far, I have spoken of the assistance given me by the colored people and teachers, but no chapter about the founding of Snow Hill Institute would be complete without a mention of Mr. R. O. Simpson, the white man on whose plantation I was reared. Mr. Simpson must have known me from my birth. I well remember that in '78 and '79 he used to stop by to see my old grandmother when riding over his plantation. I think that my grandmother prepared meals for him on some of these visits to the plantation. I also remember that after the death of grandmother, when I was sick and living with my aunt Rina, some days he would see me lying on the roadside and would toss me a coin.

On my return from Tuskegee I found Mr. Simpson deeply interested in the welfare of my people; in fact, it seemed as if he was looking for some one to start an industrial school upon his place. We had many talks together. When he found out that I had returned to cast my lot with my people, he seemed highly pleased and said that he would give a few acres for the school if I thought I could use it to advantage. I decided that this was my opportunity and told him that I could. He first gave seven acres, and then thirty-three, and finally sixty more, making in all one hundred acres that he gave the school. In later years we bought one-half of his plantation, making in all nearly two thousand acres. While all of the white people in Snow Hill have been friendly towards the

work, I have found Mr. Simpson and his entire family
to be our particular friends and I have yet to go to
them for a favor and be refused.

One of the cardinal points in Dr. Washington's
Sunday evening talks to the students and teachers at
Tuskegee was that they should buy homes of their
own. I felt that the best way to teach the people to
get a home was for me to own one myself. I thought
that it would be useless for me to talk to them about
buying homes as long as I did not have one for myself, so I secured a home.

After the school was thoroughly planted and I had
bought and paid for my home, we began to encourage
the people to buy homes. This was done through
several agencies, the Negro Farmers Conference, the
Workers Conference and the Black-Belt Improvement Society. The aim of this Society is clearly set
forth in its constitution, a part of which is as follows:

(1) This society shall be known as the Black Belt
Improvement Society. Its object shall be the general
uplift of the people of the Black Belt of Alabama; to
make them better morally, mentally, spiritually, and
financially.

(2) It shall further be the object of the Black Belt
Improvement Society as far as possible, to eliminate
the credit system from our social fabric; to stimulate
in all members the desire to raise, as far as possible,
all their food supplies at home, and pay cash for whatever may be purchased at the stores.

(3) To bring about a system of co-operation in the
purchase of what supplies cannot be raised at home
wherever it can be done to advantage.

(4) To discuss topics of interest to the communities in which the various societies may be organized, and topics relating to the general welfare of the race, and especially to farmers.

(5) To teach the people to practice the strictest economy, and especially to obtain and diffuse such information among farmers as shall lead to the improvement and diversification of crops, in order to create in farmers a desire for homes and better home conditions, and to stimulate a love for labor in both old and young. Each local organization may offer small prizes for the cleanest and best-kept house, the best pea-patch, and the best ear of corn, etc.

(6) To aid each other in sickness and in death; for this purpose a fee of ten cents will be collected from each member every month and held sacred to be used for no other purpose whatever.

(7) It shall be one of the great objects of this society to stimulate its members to acquire homes, and urge those who already possess homes to improve and beautify them.

(8) To urge our members to purchase only the things that are absolutely necessary.

(9) To exert our every effort to obliterate those evils which tend to destroy our character and our homes, such as intemperance, gambling, and social impurity.

(10) To refrain from spending money and time foolishly or in unprofitable ways; to take an interest in the care of our highways, in the paying of our taxes and the education of our children; to plant shade trees, repair our yard fences, and in general, as far as pos-

sible, bring our home life up to the highest standard of civilization.

This Society has standing committees on Government, on Education, on Business, on Housekeeping, on Labor, and on Farming. The chairman of each of these committees holds monthly meetings in the various communities, at which time various topics pertaining to the welfare and uplift of the people are discussed. As a result of these meetings the people return to their homes with new inspiration. The meetings are doing good in the communities where they are being held, and our sincere hope is that such meetings may be extended. It is the aim of the school and of its several organizations, to reach the ills that most retard the Negroes of the rural South. The articles of our simple constitution go to the very bottom of the conditions.

Thus it will be seen that the work of the class-room is only a small part of what we are trying to do for the uplift of the Negro people in the Black Belt.

CHAPTER 8.

CAMPAIGNING FOR FUNDS IN THE NORTH.

The matter of raising money for undenominational schools in the South is no easy task, and right here I ought to state just why I preferred to have such a school. Our people in the rural South are mostly Baptists and Methodists, and of course the denominations have their schools, located in certain cities. While no one is barred from these schools, it is a fact that undue influence is exerted upon the pupils to make them become members of the church that supports the school. This is not only true of the Methodist and Baptist schools, but is also true of all denominational schools in the South. I did not like that and our people do not like to have any one influence their children to join churches other than the one of their choice. We may shut our eyes to this truth, but the fact remains that Methodists do not want their children to be persuaded to join some other church, neither do the Baptists want theirs taken away from them.

Now, I wanted that my school should be free from such "isms." I wanted a school for all the Negroes, thoroughly religious in its spirit, but entirely undenominational. For twenty-five years now we have adhered strictly to this policy. Many times when all was dark and there seemed to be no way, some of these denominations would come and offer me the money to run the work, provided I would accept their faith. But this I have never done, I had rather that the work should die than to sell my principle for money. I repeat that raising money for such a school is a hard task. I have never been particularly interested as to the choice of the church that my students make, but I have been profoundly interested in their finding salvation.

A great many people to whom I appeal for aid from time to time, tell me that they give all their alms through their church. But in spite of all this, I feel that the kind of schools most needed for our people, should be broad and not narrow, deep and not shallow.

After winning the approval of the people in the community, both black and white, and getting whatever help I could from them, my thoughts turned towards the North for means to run the work. My first attempt was in March, '97. I got as far as Washington, D. C., and saw the Inauguration of President McKinley, and then I returned home.

The following June Dr. Washington wrote me to come to Tuskegee so as to accompany the Tuskegee Quartet North that summer. It must not be understood that I was one of the singers; that was not my good fortune. I was to tell what Tuskegee had done for me and was to show in turn what I was trying to do for my people. Dr. Washington reasoned in this way I would have a chance to meet some of the best people of the country and thereby gain support for my work. There was to be no collection taken for

Snow Hill, but those who became interested would often come up after the meetings and give me something for my work.

We left Tuskegee about the first of July. We spent most of the month of July in the southeastern part of Massachusetts, known as the Cape and South Shore. We had meetings at most of the churches and resorts in that section. Dr. Washington himself met us at the most prominent places.

In August we came to Boston and from there went up the North Shore. This was my first visit to Boston and it was here that I met Miss Susan D. Messinger and her brother William S. Messinger. Their home was at 81 Walnut Avenue, Roxbury, Mass. Miss Messinger had been an abolitionist. Both she and her brother were deeply interested in the welfare of my people. They listened attentively to my story and from that day became my best friends.

Although I have been going North now for twenty years, I have never met such welcome as was shown me at their home. I think I have never met such Christ-like people anywhere. It was largely through Miss Messinger's appeals in the ''Transcript'' that the people of Boston and New England learned of our work at the Snow Hill Institute. Through her appeals from time to time, we raised much money for our school. I cannot, in words, express the valuable aid these people gave us in our work. Sometimes when I had worked hard all day with poor results, I would go to their home in the evening discouraged and low-spirited, but would always find there a hearty welcome and a word of cheer. I would always leave with new zeal and fresh courage. Their home has been to me a home now for twenty years and although they are now dead, I never go to Boston but that I find time to go out to Mt. Auburn and put a fresh flower on their graves. The old home is lonely now, but the Messinger spirit still abides there in the person of Mr. Reed, their nephew. I still receive from him the hearty welcome and support that they used to give in days of old.

Another friend whom I met that summer was Mrs. J. S. Howe of Brookline (now Mrs. Herman F. Vickery). She became interested in our work through Miss Messinger and from that time to this her interest has steadily grown. Had it not been for the encouragement and aid received from the Messingers and Mrs. Howe on this trip, I am sure that I should have given up the struggle.

After leaving Boston, the Tuskegee singers went up the North Shore and on to the Isles of Shoals. There we had a very good meeting, and as Mr. Washington could not be present, I was the principal speaker. The people were greatly interested in what I said and although we took up a good collection for Tuskegee, my private collection was equally large. This the leader of the quartet did not like. It was the duty of this man who was a teacher at Tuskegee, to speak as well as myself, but for some reason he did not like to do it and would always shirk it when he could. But after this meeting he cut off my support and when we reached Portsmouth, he told me that I was dividing the interest and that he could not use me further on that trip. Of course, what little money I had been getting I had sent to the school, so I was almost penniless when he turned me off. I ought to say, however, that he gave me my fare back to Boston. I reached Boston that night about eight o'clock with no money and nowhere to go, but finally, I went to the place where we had stopped when the quartet was in Boston and I found R. W. Taylor, who at the time was financial agent in the North for Tuskegee. He saw that I was discouraged and insisted that I tell him why I had come back to Boston. When he had learned the facts he told his landlady to provide lodging and board for me at his expense until I could do better.

It was some time before Dr. Washington found out that I was not with the quartet, and as soon as he knew it, he wrote me to meet him at Lake Mohonk, N. Y. When the leader of the quartet found out that I was to be at Lake Mohonk, he tried to interfere so as to prohibit my going there, but when Dr. Washington said a thing, it had to be done, and I went to Lake Mohonk and I met the quartet again; also Dr. Washington. We had a great meeting at Lake Mohonk and after the meeting Mr. and Mrs. S. P. Avery, who were guests there, gave me $200. From here we returned South and reached Tuskeegee about the first of September. From there I returned to Snow Hill.

My trip North during the summer of '98 was very much saddened by the illness and death of my aunt Rina Rivers, whom I had learned to love as a mother, and to whom I always feel that I owe my life, for had it not been for the care she gave me during my sickness, I could not have stood the ordeal. Her death came while I was in Boston and without sufficient funds to take me either to her bed-side or to her funeral. This incident in my life has always been a cause for deep sorrow and as the years go by I feel it more keenly. I had always hoped that she could have lived until I could make her life happy, but this pleasure has been forever denied me. However she left behind four daughters and many grandchildren and I have tried to be unusually kind to them because of my great love for their mother and grandmother. Again this was a hard year because of the Spanish War and the consequent excitement.

I returned to Snow Hill early in the fall, cast down, but not destroyed. I had to adjust myself to the loss of my best earthly friend. In the meantime, our enrollment was constantly increasing and new teachers and industries were being added from year to year.

My campaign in the North during the summer of 1899 was made alone, just as the previous one had been. I got much needed experience during this summer.

In this house-to-house campaign for money, one must expect many rebuffs, but on the other hand one meets some of the finest people that have ever lived. I find, however, that as I grow older the strain is harder. I don't think that I am a very successful money raiser. However, on April 5th, 1906, at the 25th anniversary of Tuskegee, 1 delivered an address that interested Mr. Andrew Carnegie and he gave the Snow Hill Institute ten thousand dollars. (See Appendix.)

PARTIAL VIEW OF SNOW HILL INSTITUTE

CHAPTER 9.

RESULTS.

In the preceding chapters I have tried in a plain and practical way to tell the story of my life and struggle for twenty-five years. I now purpose to tell some results of this effort.

We started our work with no land, no building, and no assurance of any support from any source. In fact, we rented an old log cabin in which to begin our work. On the first day of opening, we had one teacher, three pupils and fifty cents in money, a pretty small capital with which to build a Normal and Industrial Institute. As I now look back on this early adventure of mine, I am amazed at the undertaking. Although penniless and almost without a place to rest my head, I had an abundance of hope and great faith in God. These have always been my greatest assets in this work. The people in the community were equally poor; not more than ten acres of land were owned by the colored people within a radius of ten miles, and there was even a mortgage on these ten acres. The homes of the people consisted chiefly of one-room and two-room log cabins. There was not a single glass window to be found. I remember that shortly after the founding of the school a Negro built a house and fitted it up with glass windows and people would go ten miles to see it.

The economic condition of the people was deplorable. They all carried heavy mortgages from year to year. These mortgages ranged all the way from $100 to $1500. The people were thoroughly discouraged, and seemingly had lost all hopes. Everywhere in their religious services, they sang this song: "You may have all the world, but give me Jesus." The white man was taking them at their word and giving them all of Jesus, but none of the world. So disheartened were the people that when Mr. Simpson offered to give us the first seven acres of land for the school, many tried to prevail with him not to do so, saying that they did not want any land. But as I have said, you can always find in any place a few of our people whose hearts are in the right place; it was so in this instance; a few of the old men were very stanch friends,—they stood by me in this fight and we won. Such was the condition of the people here twenty-five years ago.

Now how changed are these conditions? From the rented log cabin the school has grown until we have at present, to be exact, 1940 acres of land and twenty-four buildings, counting large and small. It enrolls each year between three and four hundred students, teaches fourteen trades, putting most stress on agriculture. The entire property is valued upwards of $125,000 and is deeded to a Board of Trustees.

But the worth of an institution is not judged by houses and land, but by its ability to serve the people among whom it is located. It has never been our end to acquire houses, land and industries, these we have used as means of enabling us to accomplish our end,

which was and still is to seek and to save that which
was lost. For twenty-five years then we have been
here, seeking lost boys, lost girls, lost men and lost
women. We have tolled our bells that they might
hear, and preached the gospel of work in order that
they might understand; we have used the church, the
Sunday-School, Bible classes and other religious societies that they might feel; the class-rooms that they
might know; the shops and farms that they might
handle and do. And so all of our material acquisi-
tions have been used to drive home one great end;
social service, better men and better women.

Now how well we have accomplished this end may
be seen from the following: Counting those who have
finished the course of study and others who have remained at the school long enough to catch its spirit
and be influenced by its teaching, we have sent out
into various parts of the South more than a thousand
young men and women who are today leading useful
and helpful lives. They are farmers, blacksmiths,
wheelwrights, carpenters, housekeepers, dressmakers,
printers, railway postal clerks, letter carriers, teachers, preachers, domestic servants, insurance agents,
doctors, expressmen, contractors, timber-inspectors,
college students. In fact, they are to be found in
every vocation known to the South. Many of these
young people have bought farms and homes of their
own, have erected neat and comfortable cottages; have
influenced their neighbors to buy land, to build better
homes, better churches and better school-houses.
They have also been instrumental in securing a higher
type of teachers and preachers. They make a special

effort always to cultivate a friendly relation between the two races. In this particular they have been remarkably successful. I shall speak more directly about their work under the chapter on Graduates. Perhaps I can in no way better show the effects of the school upon the immediate community than by referring to an address given by me and quoted in the appendix of this book.

It is the custom at Tuskegee to have each class reassemble at the school twenty years after graduation. Some one of the class is chosen by the school, to represent the class and is placed on the Commencement program. It fell my lot to represent my class on this occasion.

Of course at the anniversary of each class, that class is expected to make a donation to the school. Although this had been the custom for several years, the class donations very seldom amounted to more than $100. Sometimes they were as small as $25.00 or less. Somehow I have always felt that the graduates of Tuskegee owed that institution a debt of gratitude which they can never pay, and thought that they should make the class anniversaries mean something more substantial to the school than they had meant. So long before our time came, I wrote the members of my class telling them that it should be our aim to give Tuskegee $1000 at our Anniversary. They readily agreed with me and the class set itself to the task of raising the $1000. This was done because we felt that the time had come for the graduates to give more substantial aid to their Alma-Mater, and as a stimulus to those who are to follow. I think in a small way

A NEWER TYPE OF HOME IN THE BLACK BELT

it has served that purpose, because these class anniversary donations have never been less than $500 since that date.

I think of all the talks I have ever made, none have given me the real joy that this one gave. I feel that this was true for the reason that this was a giving talk rather than a receiving one. The address is also given in the appendix.

CHAPTER 10.

ORIGIN OF THE JEANES FUND.

In the fall of 1902 I received a letter from Dr. Washington requesting me to speak at a meeting in Philadelphia in the interest of Tuskegee. Miss Cornelia Bowen, also a graduate of Tuskegee, was asked to speak at the same meeting. We both accepted. During my stay in the city Mr. Henry C. Davis, a trustee of Tuskegee at the time, gave me a letter of introduction to Miss Anna T. Jeanes, a wealthy woman who seldom gave to schools as large as Tuskegee and Hampton, but who would, in all probability, be interested in my school.

In going to Miss Jeanes's home on Arch Street I had many apprehensions but I found her very cordial and deeply interested in the welfare of my people. I told her of my struggle to get an education and how, after finishing at Tuskegee I had returned to my home in Alabama. I described the condition of the public schools in the rural districts. She gave keen interest to this part of my story. Finally, she asked me if I was aiming to build a large school such as Tuskegee or Hampton. I told her that I had no such idea; that I only wanted to build a school that could properly care for three or four hundred students, and try as best I could to help the little schools throughout that section. When I returned to Snow Hill I found a check from her for five thousand dollars for the work at Snow Hill.

Each year after this Miss Jeanes gave me from $300 to $2000 for the work at Snow Hill. Finally, in the fall of 1906 when she had moved to the home in Germantown which she had established for the aged, I called to see her. She was then ill and although the nurse said that I could not see her, after my card had been taken to her, she sent for me. She was quite feeble, but said to me: "I have been deeply interested in what thee has been telling me all these years about the little schools. I would give largely to them if thee thinks that thee could get Dr. Washington or Dr. Frissell to come to see me." I am sure she was thinking of the large experience of those men. She said also that she thought if she would make such a gift as she contemplated, it might induce other great philanthropists to do as much.

At my suggestion Dr. Washington visited Miss Jeanes who gave $11,000 each to Dr. Washington and Dr. Frissell to be used as they thought best for the small schools.

I am positive that the Jeanes Fund originated in this way, and I am proud of the part that I had in this affair and that so many Negro children can be helped by the fund that is destined to do so much for the elevation of our people in this country.

CHAPTER 11.

APPRECIATION.

In building up an institution such as we have done at Snow Hill, no one man is entitled to all the credit. On the contrary, it is impossible to name all to whom credit is due. We can only speak of those who have been closely allied with us and whose work has been prominent in the building of the institution. Perhaps of these, the Trustees come first. We could never have gone on with the work from year to year without their aid and assistance.

Without Mr. R. O. Simpson there could not have been any Snow Hill Institute. We might have built a similar school elsewhere, but we could not have built it at Snow Hill. Mr. Simpson gave the first site for the school and from the start has been one of our best friends. He stood for Negro Education when it was unpopular for him to do so. He allied himself with this cause, at the risk of being ostracised by other white people. Because of his firm stand, most of the white people in this section have been won over to his way of thinking, and now there is scarcely if any opposition hereabouts to the Snow Hill Institute.

Mr. R. O. Simpson is one of the noblest men that I have ever met, North or South. He is absolutely free from all racial and petty prejudice that we so often

find in the average man of today. I feel safe in saying that he is living at least fifty years ahead of his
time. The things that he stands for and have been
fighting for, for thirty years, are coming more and
more to pass, and although it seems hard for the present generation to accept them, they must be accepted
if we would make the world safe for Democracy. He
is a true patriot, a true democrat, and a zealous Christian gentleman. Mr. Simpson has a family of five
children, three sons and two daughters, all of whom
possess his spirit to a large degree.

I first met Rev. R. C. Bedford at Tuskegee while I
was there in school. I loved him from the first time
I saw him and I feel that this was because of his deep
and sincere interest in our people. Until I met Mr.
Bedford, I had always distrusted the white man and
thought it was impossible for any white man to be
free from race prejudice. After my graduation at
Tuskegee, as I said before, I returned to Snow Hill
and seeing that Mr. Bedford and Mr. Simpson had
something in common, arranged to have Mr. Bedford
come to Snow Hill and meet Mr. Simpson. Their
meeting resembled that of Jonathan and David, and I
believe their friendship was equally great. It continued until Mr. Bedford's death. Mr. Bedford was one
man who understood what it was to build up an institution from nothing. He knew the hardships one
had to undergo to meet bills when there was no money
appropriated for these bills. He knew what it was
to make brick without straw. Ofttimes when the burden was heavy and the yoke rough, it was the encouraging words from Mr. Bedford that gave me strength

and courage to continue. While his particular mission was to look after the Tuskegee schools, he loved every good work and would always lend a hand to a good cause. He was thoroughly imbued with the Christ-spirit.

I cannot express in words the great debt of gratitude that I owe the immortal Booker T. Washington, for I owe all to him. It was he who changed my view of life. He changed me from the visionary to the substantial, from the shadow to the substance, from the artificial to the real, and from words to deeds. Dr. Washington became a trustee of Snow Hill Institute from its beginning and remained as such until his death. He made three visits to Snow Hill, the last being November 18th, 1914. Dr. Washington always did what he could to help us in our work. He seemed to appreciate the efforts that we were putting forth to uplift our people. He could sympathize with us; he could understand that an institution that had no permanent support, but had to depend upon the efforts of one man to raise money, could not be perfect, and many things were not as well as they should be. Dr. Washington could sympathize with us because he knew what it was. He had borne the burden in the heat of the day. But I find that persons who have done nothing themselves, but have lived as parasites most of their days, are much more critical than Dr. Washington ever could be. Sometimes I am asked to what I attribute Dr. Washington's success in life. My answer to this question has always been the same: to his spirit and simplicity. He possessed in a very large degree, the spirit and simplicity of the Master. He never struck back. He always sought to do good to those who would do evil to him. He was meek and lowly of heart, and I know that he has found rest for his soul.

There are other trustees who have played a prominent part in the development of the work here, among whom may be mentioned Mr. James H. Post, Rev. Henry Wilder Foote, Prof. William Howell Reed and Mr. William H. Baldwin, 3rd. The trustees are now taking a more active part in the work than ever before. This is their bounden duty, because the school is theirs, not mine.

Next to the Trustees, the officers and teachers have played a prominent part in the work here. My classmate, Henry A. Barnes, has been treasurer of the school for twenty-three years, which period of service is, in itself, a tribute to his faithfulness. Mr. Barnes not only does the work of treasurer, but is also Acting Principal during my absence from the school, and under him the work of the school continues with little or no interruption while I am away. What Mr. Barnes has been to the Financial Department, Mr. R. A. Daly has been to our Industries. I consider Mr. Daly the best Industrial man that we can have.

The Academic Department has been developed under the management of Messrs. Whitehead and Handy, and it stands well in comparison with that of other similar schools in the State.

I cannot overestimate the value of the conscientious work done by my secretaries during all these years. Miss Rebecca Savage (now Mrs. R. V. Cooke) served in this capacity for fourteen years and Miss O. H.

Williamson has served one way or another for five years. Much of the office work and responsibility fall upon the secretaries and this responsibility they have borne without complaint. Sometimes we have been compelled to work night and day, but they have always been willing to serve. Not only have the officers been willing to serve, but the rank and file of our teachers have shown the same spirit of willingness from year to year. Sometimes they would get their pay promptly and at other times they would have to wait for months, but always they have been willing to do what they could to cheer and help me in the darkest hour of the struggle. I believe that the spirit of the officers and teachers of Snow Hill Institute is: "Not to be ministered unto, but to minister."

Aside from Trustees, officers and teachers, there is that great cloud of witnesses which no man can number, who have helped by their aid, their words of cheer and their presence from time to time. These are in all parts of the country, but principally in the North and East. How shall we thank them for what they have been to us? We cannot do it by words, because there are no words that could adequately express our deep sense of gratitude to this host of friends. We must, therefore, be contented to show them by our acts and deeds that we are ever mindful of their help and that each day we are striving more and more to make ourselves and our work worthy of their aid and encouragement. Among this cloud of witnesses are some of the best people that God has ever made. They deem it a privilege to give and to help the lowly.

TYPICAL LOG CABIN IN THE BLACK BELT

HOME OF A SNOW HILL GRADUATE

In speaking of our debt of gratitude to the forces that have helped in building up our work here, we must not overlook the press. There are certain great papers in this country that have been fearless in their advocacy of right and justice to the Negro, and have always opened their columns to any cause that has for its end the uplift of the lowly. Among these may be mentioned especially *The New York Evening Post, The Boston Transcript, The Springfield Republican, The Hartford Courant,* and in the South *The Montgomery Advertiser.*

One also receives much aid and encouragement from those who are in similar work. It has been my good fortune to meet in the North from time to time with those who have similar work as mine. In this way I have met most of the Principals of Southern Schools. Perhaps Mr. W. H. Holtzclaw of Utica, Mississippi, comes first in this class. This is true, because I have known him the longest. I first met him in Tuskegee in the early nineties, when we both were in school there. His life was similar to mine, as we both had a very hard time in trying to get an education. I became interested in him there and when he finished I took him to work with me at Snow Hill. It was at Snow Hill that he met and married Miss Mary Ella Patterson, one of our teachers. They remained with us at Snow Hill four years. Both Mr and Mrs. Holtzclaw have always seemed more like my relatives than like friends. Some of Mr. Holtzclaw's best teachers today are graduates of Snow Hill Institute. I have always been deeply interested in the welfare of Utica for it is in reality an outgrowth of Snow Hill.

Other Principals whom I meet occasionally, are President Battle of Okolona, Mississippi, where a number of our graduates have worked. I have found Mr. Battle interested in the general cause of Negro Education, and too, we found in our case that the cause is the same. I have had occasion to ask Mr. Battle just how our graduates measure up with his other teachers, and he tells me that Snow Hill graduates are among his best helpers. By this I know that in deeds, not words, we are making good.

Another most interesting character whom I always meet on my tours North is Mr. Frank P. Chisholm, Financial Secretary of Tuskegee Institute. I have been knowing Mr. Chisholm for a great many years. We have attended the Summer School at Harvard several summers together and it has been both a pleasure and benefit to me to be associated with him in this way. Although working directly for Tuskegee, he has always been willing to speak a word for Snow Hill wherever the opportunity presented itself. I have obtained many suggestions from Mr. Chisholm which have been very beneficial to me in my work here. I consider Mr. Chisholm a representative type of the new Negro of to-day. He is a brilliant scholar, a clear thinker, and is doing a very effective work for Tuskegee.

Others with whom I come in contact on such trips are Principal Hunt of Fort Valley, Ga.; Principal Minafee of Denmark, S. C.; Principal Long of Christianburg, Va. These young men and many others are doing a greater work than they know, and all possess in a smaller or larger degree the spirit of dear old Tuskegee. They are all preaching the gospel of Service.

CHAPTER 12.

GRADUATES AND EX-STUDENTS.

Prof. Bagley in his "Classroom Management," page 225, has the following to say in "Testing Results":

"The ultimate test of efficiency of efforts is the result of effort. Unhappily this test is seldom applied to the work of teaching. We judge the teacher by the process rather than by the product, and we introduce a number of extraneous criteria to hide the absence of a real criterion. We watch the way in which he conducts a recitation, how many slips he makes in his diction and syntax, inspect his personal appearance, ask of what school he is a graduate and how many degrees he possesses, inquire into his moral character, determine his church membership, and judge him to be a good or a poor teacher according to our findings. All of these queries may have their place in the estimation of any teacher's worth, but they do not strike the most salient, the most vital, point at issue. That point is simply this: Does he 'make good' in results? Does he do the thing that he sets out to do, and does he do it well?"

I agree wholly with Prof. Bagley in this particular and on these grounds we are willing to stand or fall by the results of our graduates.

Speaking of our graduates and ex-students, I wish

to point to the life and work of a few written by their own hands because in these particular cases I can testify to the truth of every word they say, having known them from early childhood. Their record follows and they speak for themselves:

"I was born in Snow Hill, Wilcox County, Alabama, about 30 years ago. I was the 14th child of a family of 17. My father was a very prosperous farmer and believed in educating his children. Each year he would send them by twos off to schools, such as Talladega, Tuskegee and Normal, Alabama. Some of the older children, however, did not take advantage of the great opportunity they had. He spent his money lavishly on them and about the time I was large enough to go off to school, he was not as prosperous. As soon as I was old enough he kept me in the public and sometimes private schools, both summer and winter. Yet, he had promised to send the remainder of us off to school. Fortunately for us, however, Snow Hill Institute had been established by Mr. W. J. Edwards, and my father being very much impressed with Mr. Edwards and his teachers, consulted him about entering three children, I being the youngest. Mr. Edwards kindly consented and we were at once put in school there. I was also fond of music and after learning that Snow Hill Institute had such an efficient music teacher, I was very much pleased to attend school there. So in the year of 1900 I entered. I was enabled to develop my musical talent to the extent that I was selected to play for my home church, and that inspired other students to attend Snow Hill Institute.

"During my first year in school there I was undecided as to just what I was going to follow as a trade.
I worked awhile in the sewing room then in the laun-
dry—was also interested in cooking and took special
lessons in cooking under Miss Mabry. In fact, I
studied cooking the first two years. Finally, in my
senior year, Miss C. V. Johnson, then Secretary to
Mr. Edwards, asked me to clean the offices of morn-
ings for her and work with her on my work days. I
began this work and would watch her using the type-
writer so much until I fully decided that I wanted to
make an efficient secretary for someone, and began
working to that end. On my work days she would
have me copying letters with ink. I would be careful
not to make a mistake. During the time I was working in the office, Mr. Edwards would often send me on
errands and tell me to see how quickly I could go and
come. He seemed to have been very much impressed
with my work as a student in both the Academic and
Industrial departments. There were several prize
contests given my class by different teachers, and I
won each prize. This was in the Academic department. There were twelve members in the class. Mr.
Edwards had the members of my class to write some
friends of the school for scholarships (this being the
request of the friends) and of the two persons that
received favorable answers, I was one. During the
whole time I was in school I did not receive one de-
merit, or a black mark. Our teachers seemed perfect,
and it was a pleasure for me to try to please them.
"In the year 1903 I graduated from the institution
with a splendid grasp of all that the school stood for

and in favor with all of my teachers and friends. Mr. Edwards, knowing my ability to do things as I was instructed, employed me to work in his office as clerk. I then put forth more strenuous efforts to do efficient work and would try to improve myself along that particular line of work. So in the summer of 1905 I attended school at Cheyney, Pa., taking a special course in English, typewriting and shorthand. I did my best to give satisfaction in my work.

"In the year 1909 I was made Private Secretary to Mr. Edwards and a member of the Executive Council. I still had a desire to make further improvement, and in the summer of 1911, I attended Comer's Commercial College in Boston, Mass., trying to become more efficient in the work that was assigned to my hands. Principal Edwards would have to be away from the school most of the time soliciting means to carry on the work, but I tried to not leave a stone unturned in accomplishing the work he left behind. Snow Hill Institute succeeded in inculcating into my life a love for work, and I am not satisfied unless I have some work to do.

"I worked for Mr. Edwards untiringly until October, 1917. I was married, however, in July, 1917. I have often wondered where my lot would have been cast had there been no Snow Hill Institute."

"I was born of ex-slave parents on the Calhoun plantation in Dallas County, Alabama. I am not quite sure of the exact date of my birth, but at any rate, as nearly as I have been able to learn, I was born near the village called Richmond, in the month of May, 1883. My life had its beginning under the most difficult circumstances. This was so, however, not because of any wilful neglect on the part of my parents, but as ex-slaves they naturally knew but little as to the providing for the maintenance of their family and home. I was born in a one-room log cabin about 14 x 15 feet square. In this cabin I lived with my mother, father and the other eight sisters and brothers until providentially I found an opportunity to enter school at Snow Hill Institute, Snow Hill, Alabama.

"I went to Snow Hill in the year of 1896, and there remained for eight years receiving instruction at the hand of a loyal band of self-sacrificing teachers, who not only taught me how to read, write and to cipher, but in addition they taught me lessons of thrift and industry which have proven to be the main saving point in my life.

"I completed the prescribed course of study at the Snow Hill Institute in 1904 and returned home as I had resolved to do, before entering school there, for the purpose of helping the people of my home community.

"The Street Manual Training School (Incorporated) at Richmond, Dallas County, Alabama, was started in 1904 with one teacher, fifteen pupils and no money. Since that time it has grown to the point where it now has thirty acres of land, four buildings, and an enrollment of three hundred pupils. The entire property is valued at fifteen thousand dollars ($15,000) and deeded to a board of Trustees. Among the members of this board are: Mr. J. D. Alison, President, Mrs. Edwin D. Mead, the Rev. Mr. Emmanuel M.

Brown, Mr. Wm. D. Brigham, Mr. Walter Powers,
Mr. Edwin W. Lambert, Mr. W. J. Edwards, Mrs.
Francis Carr and Mr. Henry A. Barnes.

"This school is training some three hundred Negro
children between the ages of six and eighteen years
in the practical arts necessary to enable them to make
an earnest, comfortable living. There is no attempt
made to teach them foreign languages, either dead or
living; but they are well grounded in the English language. They do not study higher mathematics, but
they learn simple arithmetic. They spend no time on
psychology, economics, sociology, or logic; their time
is taken up trying to raise crops, to manage a small
farm, to cook and to sew."

SKETCH OF MY LIFE.

"I was born in Snow Hill, Wilcox County, Alabama,
December 24th, 1883. My parents were Emanuel and
Emma McDuffie. I was brought up under the most
adverse conditions. My father died about six months
before my birth, thus leaving my mother with the care
of seven children. As I had never seen my father, I
was often referred to by the other children of the
community, as the son of "none." In July, 1893, my
mother died and the burden of caring for the children
then fell upon my old grandmother, who was known
throughout the community as "Aunt" Polly. In order
to help secure food and clothing for myself and the
rest of the family, I was compelled to plow an ox on
a farm and as we usually made from four to five bales
of cotton and 40 and 50 bushels of corn each year, she

was looked upon as a great farmer. When I was fifteen years of age, my grandmother was called to her heavenly rest, thus leaving a house full of children to shift for themselves. After her death I became interested in education and immediately applied for admittance to Snow Hill Normal and Industrial Institute, which had recently been established. I was admitted as a work student, working all day and attending school about two hours and a half at night. Until I entered Snow Hill Institute, I had a very vague idea about life as it pertained to the Negro. In fact, up until that time, I was of the opinion that the Negro had no business being anything; but after entering the school and being surrounded by a different atmosphere and seeing what had already been accomplished by Mr. Edwards, I soon realized that the Negro had as much right to life and liberty as any other man.

"While it was great joy for me to be in school, I was woefully unprepared to remain there. Really, I am unable to tell the many obstacles that confronted me while in school. But one of my many difficulties was to get sufficient clothing, for when I entered, I had on all that I possessed and day after day I wore what I had until finally they got beyond mending. The teachers at Snow Hill were just as they are now, extremely hard against dirt and filth. As I only had one suit of underwear and as we were compelled to change at least once a week, I could plainly see that my condition was becoming more alarming each day. So I would go down to the spring at night, wash that suit and dry it the best I could by the heater that was

in my room. Quite often I would go for days wearing
damp or wet underwear, which has caused both
pain and doctor bills in after years. Finally, Mr.
Edwards relieved me of this situation when he sent
me to the sales-room to get a pair of second-hand
trousers and another suit of underwear. My trousers
didn't begin to fit, for they were both too large and
too long, but I wore them with pleasure because I
went to Snow Hill in search of an education and I was
willing to make any sacrifice to obtain my desire.
Through all of my troubles I never became discouraged, because I felt that some day I would be prepared to be of service to my people.

"Of all things that gave me inspiration while in
school, Mr. Edwards's own Christian life which he
lived before us day after day had more to do with
keeping me there than anything else. His courage and
perseverance under difficulties, which we all could see,
were noble lessons to me. In his Sunday evening talks
in the chapel, he would plead with us to shape our
lives for work among those who were less fortunate
than we. One Sunday evening, he made a powerful
and vivid appeal, admonishing the students to go out,
when they had finished their education, and start their
life's work among the lowly in the rural districts. He
spoke these words many times during the term. In
fact, so often did he repeat them that the very
thoughts of them inspired me and I soon learned to
love the cause of humanity as well and as dearly as
did Mr. Edwards himself. Soon after completing my
course in May, 1904, a call came from the Black Belt
of North Carolina for a man to go to Laurinburg and

build up an Industrial school there. After talking
the matter over with Mr. Edwards, I decided to go.
"I reached the town of Laurinburg September 15,
1904. When I got there I found that the people had
been so often deceived and hoodwinked by political
demagogues and supposed race leaders, that they had
no confidence in any one. But I made a start and
opened school in an old public school building with
seven students and fifteen cents in cash. As the people had no confidence in me, it was hard for me to increase my enrollment, but I continued to labor with
them on the streets and in the churches until I gradually won their respect. Then we started the erection
of a new school building and from that day until now,
both white and black have taken the deepest interest
in the work and we now have the absolute confidence
of all the people.

"The work has constantly grown from year to year
and results have been obtained. From one teacher,
seven students and fifteen cents in cash, thirteen years
ago, the institution now has fourteen teachers, upwards of four hundred students from all over North
Carolina, Virginia, South Carolina and Georgia, and
counting land, livestock, five large and three small
buildings, it has a property valuation of $30,000 all
free of debt. Each year our teachers are selected
from some of the best schools of the South; such as
Tuskegee Institute, Shaw University, Snow Hill Institute, Claflin University, Benedict College, etc.
Eight industries are taught, consisting of farming,
blacksmithing, wheelwrighting, sewing, laundering,
printing, domestic science and home nursing.

"We are kept in immediate need of money for current and building expenses, but we are going on accomplishing results with what we have at hand. Boys and girls are being sent out each year to work among their fellows. These young men and women are reaching the masses and as a result, the moral tone of the people is being aroused to the contemplation of higher ideals and they are at last becoming serious as to the sober side of life. Excursions, parties and a good time generally are slowly but surely being relegated to the rear. Our farmers are studying how to become better farmers and in all walks of life, we are improving in workshop and the various industries.

"Verily, the school room is doing much in awakening the dormant energies of the Negro for good. In fact, the school's influence is helping the people generally. Where there were ignorance and indifference, now we have a fair measure of intelligence and thrift. The people are buying homes and property, and in many ways showing signs of aspiration.

"We have also organized a farmers' conference and it is gratifying indeed to see how hundreds of farmers, with their wives and children, turn out seeking information, demonstration and co-operation. I have been thus enabled to help my people here in North Carolina by giving them the new truth and the new light and pointing them on to a better way."

Waverley Turner Carmichael was born at Snow Hill, Ala., in 1888, and was reared on the farm as all country negro boys are. All of his education was obtained at the Snow Hill Institute except for six weeks he spent in the Harvard Summer School last year.

GRADUATES OF SNOW HILL INSTITUTE

EMMANUEL McDUFFIE, Principal Laurinburg Normal and Industrial Institute,
Laurinburg, N. C.

JOHN W. BRISTER, who established a prize
at Snow Hill Institute.

REV. EMMANUEL M. BROWN of Street Manual
Training School, Richmond, Alabama.

WAVERLEY TURNER CARMICHAEL, Poet of
Snow Hill.

I had been deeply impressed with the poems which he had been writing for several years, but as I was no judge of poems, I thought I would give him a chance to bring his poems before those who could judge, so I received for him a free scholarship at the Summer School at Harvard. He read his poems to the class on several occasions and I had the opportunity of hearing him several times. They had a deep impression upon the class, so much so that his professor wrote the introduction to his book in the following words:—

"When Waverley Carmichael, as a student in my summer class at Harvard, brought me one day a modest sheaf of his poems, I felt that in him a race had become or at least was becoming articulate. We have had, it is true, sympathetic portrayals of Negro life and feeling from without; we have had also the poems of Dunbar, significant of the high capabilities of the Negro as he advances far along the way of civilization and culture. The note which is sounded in this little volume is of another sort. These humble and often imperfect utterances have sprung up spontaneously from the soul of a primitive and untutored folk. The rich emotion, the individual humor, the simple wisdom, the naive faith which are its birthright, have here for the first time found voice. It is sufficient to say of Waverley Carmichael that he is a full blooded southern Negro, that until last summer he has never been away from his native Alabama, that he has had but the most limited advantages of education, and that he has shared the portion of his race in hardship, poverty and toil. He does not know why he wrote these poems. It is an amazing thing that he should have done so—a freak, we may call it, of the wind of genius, which bloweth where it listeth and singles out one in ten thousand to find a fitting speech for the dumb thought and feeling of the rest.

But we need not base the claim of Carmichael to the attention of the public merely on considerations of this sort. His work speaks for itself. It is original and sincere. It follows no traditions and suffers no affectation. It is artless, yet it reaches the goal of art. The rhythms, especially of some of the religious pieces, are of a kind which is beyond the reach of effort. He has rightly called them melodies. Occasionally there is, it seems to me, a touch of something higher, as in the haunting refrain of the lyric "Winter is Coming."

> De yaller leafs are falling fas'
> Fur summer days is been and pas'
> The air is blowin' mighty cold,
> Like it done in days of old.

But this is rare. Oftenest the characteristic note is humor, or tender melancholy relieved by a philosophy of cheer and courage, and the poetic virtue is that of simple truth. We are reminded of no poet so strongly as of Burns.

What Waverley Carmichael may accomplish in the future I do not know. But certainly in this volume he has entitled himself to the gratitude of his own race and to the sympathetic appreciation of all who have its interests and those of true poetry at heart."

JAMES HOLLY HANFORD.

Mr. William Stanley Braithwaite speaking of his poems had the following to say:

"Many have claimed the mantle of Paul Laurence Dunbar, but only upon the shoulders of Waverley Turner Carmichael has it fallen, and he wears it with becoming grace and fitness. For this poet, a veritable child of Negro folk, gives expression to its spirit in need and language more akin to the ante-bellum 'spirituel' than any writer I know. Like those 'black and unknown bards' he sings because he must, with all their fervid imaginativeness, symbolizations, poignant strains of pathos and philosophic humor."

Mr. Braithwaite is the best known Negro critic of poetry in the world today.

As for me who has always lived in the South and know the Southern Negro through and through, I feel and believe that Carmichael has interpreted Negro life as never before.

We hope and pray that Carmichael will live through this great ordeal and come back to us and continue his work of interpreting Negro life.

There are hundreds of other graduates and ex-students who have won distinction in other fields and are doing equally as well as those who have been mentioned here. We have their record at the school, and any one can have them for the asking. I only wish to mention in a brief way two other graduates because they have established a first and second prize at Snow Hill. They are John W. Brister and Edmond J. O'Neal.

Several years ago the late Misses Collins (Ellen and Marguerite) of New York, two of the most sainted women whom I ever met, established an annual prize at the school known as the Sumner Peace Prize, of $15.00. But at their death this prize would have stopped unless some one had taken it up. Both Mr. Brister and Mr. O'Neal had won these prizes several times while they were in school. So at the death of the Misses Collins they came forward and said that they would be responsible for the prize each year on condition that the school make a first and second prize instead of one, Mr. Brister giving $10.00 in gold for the first prize and Mr. O'Neal giving $5.00 in gold for the second. This they have done for several years, and they constantly assure me that it will be kept up during their lifetime. This shows that our graduates are carrying with them the spirit of Christ, "Freely receive, freely give."

CHAPTER 13.

THE SOLUTION OF THE NEGRO PROBLEM.

All prophecies pertaining thus far to the solution of the Negro Problem have failed. Men in all parts of the country are becoming alarmed over the situation and are asking, "whither are we drifting?" And yet although everyone admits that there is a Negro problem, few are agreed as to the exact nature of the problem, and still fewer are agreed as to what the final answer should be.

Generally speaking, the Negro problem consists of twelve millions of people of African descent living in this country, mostly in the Southern states, and forming one-third of the population of this section and one-eighth of the entire population of the United States. Notwithstanding the fact that we are far from an agreement as to the answer to this problem, we are all agreed that the solution must be sought in the answers to the following questions: What is to be the economic, the political, the civil, and the social status of the Negro in this country?

It is true that there are criminals in the Negro race for whom no legal form of punishment is too severe. It is also true that the better and best classes of Negroes are daily being insulted in the streets, on the street-cars, on the railroads, at the ticket offices, at the baggage rooms, the express offices, and in fact, in all places pertaining to public travel. They are persecuted, despised, rejected, and discriminated against before every court in the South. Since the Negro is now being lynched as readily for his sins of omission as he is for his sins of commission, it is quite necessary for him when traveling in the South, to keep constantly in telegraphic communication with the agent at the station ahead as to the movement of the mob. In addition to this, the Negro is subjected to many other forms of persecution and discrimination in almost every walk of life. These things go to make up what we call the Negro problem.

The White Man's Solution.

A large majority of the white men in the South believe that this problem is to be solved by the Negro "learning his place" and keeping in it. Though they do not say just what this place is, they purpose to teach it to the Negro by disfranchisement, by limiting his education, by discrimination on the streets and on the railroads, by barring him from public parks, public libraries, and public amusements of any kind, by insulting replies to courteous questions, by conviction for trivial offences, and, finally, by judge lynch and the shot gun. This class is called the rabble.

There is another class of white men in the South, though fewer in number, who deprecate all such views and actions (as advanced by this first class). They believe that the Negro should have equal legal rights, but that he should be denied equal political and educational rights. They believe the Bible to be the panacea for all the ills of the Negro. To bear out their contention, they often revert to the time when, they say, there was no race problem. This, they say, was during slavery, when the master taught his slaves the beneficent influence of the Holy Bible. They are now appealing to the white men of the South to return to this practice. In this class would fall a large number of politicians, statesmen, educators, and ministers. This is called the conservative class.

There is still a third class of white men in the South, who believe that the Negro is a man, nothing more and nothing less. They believe that under similar circumstances the Negro will act as other races do. They contend that the Negro should have equal rights in every respect; they believe that worthy Negroes like worthy white men, should vote, and that ignorant and vicious Negroes like ignorant and vicious white men, should not; that the school money should be divided equally among the children of the state regardless of race, color or previous conditions; that the Negro should be given justice in all of the courts; that the criminal and lawless Negro, like the criminal and lawless white man, should be punished to the full extent of the law. They believe that a strict adherence to this view will result in the final solution of the problem. There are, however, so few who feel in this way, and they are so widely scattered, that they can hardly be called a class. The other classes of white people consider them insane and accuse them of advocating social equality. They are given no voice in the government and their wishes are disregarded as

readily as those of the Negro. They are sometimes
persecuted, ostracised, and harmed in every conceivable way. This class is increasing and the two other
classes decreasing.

The Negro's Method of Solution.

There are three classes of Negroes in the South, but
only one desires a solution of the problem and that is
class number two, of those I shall mention. Class
number one is composed chiefly of the illiterate and
superstitious Negroes. They usually work on the
railroads, on the steamboats, in the large saw-mills,
and on the farms for wages. They have no homes and
do not want any; but float from place to place. This
class is contented to be let alone, but is quick to resent
an insult, and will shoot almost as readily as the white
man, and make no attempt to choose their victims.
Among this class are to be found the whiskey seller, the
drunkard, the gambler, and the criminal of the lowest
type. It is the low, degraded and depraved criminals
of this class who stir up and incite race hatred, which
always results in race riots. They do not attend
church or any other religious meeting. The better
class of Negroes are as anxious to get rid of these as
the white man.

The second class is composed of the renters of
farms, the owners of farms, of homes, of preachers,
teachers, students, professional and business men.
They believe that the Negro should be educated in the
trades as well as in the professions; that they should
own homes, pay their taxes and perform their civic du-

ties like all other citizens and that they should possess
all of the rights and privileges that are delegated to
them by the Constitution of the United States. They
believe in the purity of the state and in the sanctity of
the home. They are enduring, self-sacrificing, pa-
tient, and long suffering, and desire the good of all.
It is this class that always assists in quelling race riots
and is constantly seeking the co-operation of the best
class of white people in order that the relation between
the races may be of the most cordial nature. It is this
class also who do not lose their heads though innocent
members of the race be murdered by the mob. Though
this class is rapidly increasing, it is still far inferior
in number to the first class.

The third class is composed chiefly of the ante-bellum Negroes. They are well advanced in age and are
contented with their present lot. Many of them have
waited for years for the forty acres and mule and having been disappointed in their expectation, they have
lost all hopes. They are fast losing sight on the things
of this world and gaining sight on the things of the
world to come. Ofttimes, they sing, "You may have
all this world, but give me Jesus." They are perfectly harmless and have no earthly ambition. This is
what the white man here calls a good Negro; for him
they act as pall-bearers when he dies and for him they
weep when he is gone. In many instances they erect
monuments to his memory.

Fallacy of the Master and the Bible Remedy.

Since the recent riots that have occurred in Georgia,
North Carolina, Tennessee, Arkansas and other South-

ern States, many white ministers and other prominent
citizens of the South have been advocating a return to
the master and Bible theory of slavery days, when,
they say, there was no race problem. But every student of history knows that at the same time the master
was carrying the Bible to his slaves this country was
struggling with one of the greatest race problems that
the world has ever witnessed and the slavery phase of
this problem was settled by one of the bloodiest wars
in the annals of history. Furthermore, the student of
history knows that the master carried the lash more
often to the slave's back than the Bible to the slave's
heart; that the lash kept the slave in subjection.

If the relation between the races now seems most
strained and the solution of the problem seems farther away than ever, we must be candid and seek the
cause of failure in the methods that we have been
using. In the past, the white man's idea of the solution has been contrary to the Negro's idea. The white
man has been trying to circumscribe the Negro's
sphere, at the same time, the Negro has been trying to
know the truth which would make him free; yet, both
claim to be trying to solve the same problem. Before a satisfactory solution of the problem can be had,
it will be necessary for the best white people and the
best class of Negroes to get together and agree as to
what the solution must be. Is it to consist of the Negro knowing his place and staying in it, or is it to
consist of the Negro knowing the truth and being
free? Which shall it be? Unless they can agree as to
the answer there can be no satisfactory solution.

In a democratic form of government having one

language, one history, one literature, one religion, one
Bible, and one God, there can be only one man who is
the sum total of these, only one man who is the typi-
cally good democratic citizen, and this man will be
known by his accomplishments and not by the color
of his skin. If we should have two types, two men,
then we must have two governments, two languages,
two histories, two literatures, two religions, two Bi-
bles, and two Gods.

If the shiftless, ignorant, superstitious, and criminal class of Negroes is increasing, it is because the
ruling class of white men have been limiting his education, disfranchising him, and in other ways trying
to doom him to serfdom. The great race riot in Atlanta was simply the culmination of the ten months'
campaigning of race hatred. Men who are now writing resolutions and sound and sane editorials, were
then rivaling each other in their abuse of the Negro.
The nominee for governor seemingly, was to be given
to the one who could prove himself the greatest enemy
of the Negro. It is a divine and immutable law that
if we sow the wind we will reap the whirlwind.

Only One Road to the Solution.

Lynchings and mobs will not solve the problem, for
it has been proven that such actions beget crimes. De-
priving him of educational advantages and disfranchising him, will not suffice, for on the one hand this
method produces ignorant Negroes, and on the other
hand it increases in the white man the belief that the
Negro has no rights which a white man is bound to

respect. These two states of mind in the last analysis will always produce crime. The master and Bible theory will not solve it, because the criminal and lawless Negro does not attend church. There is but one true solution and that lies in compulsory education for all the children of the state with religious, moral and industrial training. If the South is sincere in its efforts to help the Negro, or even if the ministers and other citizens who are now filling the daily press with suggestions as to the practical solution of this problem are sincere, they will advocate the enacting of compulsory educational laws and see to it that all children between the ages of six and fourteen are kept in school. They will also advocate a more equitable division of the school fund between the races. The great factor in the solution of this problem is education and the Negro schools are the hope of the race.

The Attitude of the North Towards This Problem.

Just now, the attitude of the North towards this problem is that of an onlooker and well wisher. For a number of years the South has been saying to the North, "Hands off, we understand the Negro and we can solve our own problem." The North, seemingly, has heeded this injunction and the press and politicians of the North, barring a few, have been inclined to take sides with the so-called conservative class of white men of the South.

The philanthropist of the North, however, while being a friend to the white South has been none the less a friend to the black South, and has kept constantly

aiding Negro education and it is the schools thus supported that are doing the most effective work in the
uplifting of the race. It was the wise guidance, judi-
cious and calm leadership of the men in these schools
that saved the day at Atlanta. All of these schools
have the record of their graduates and ex-students
opened to the public for inspection. And an impartial
inspection of these records will show that these students and graduates have made since leaving school,
according to their circumstances, as creditable a mark
as the graduates and ex-students from any of our
Northern schools. These schools do not give college
training.

In these perilous times when the race is passing
through such trying ordeals, and when the souls of
men are being tried, I trust that our friends will not
forsake us. Our industrial schools and colleges and
the better element of the race, need their sympathy,
encouragement, and assistance now as never before.
My prayer is for a double portion of their spirit and
an increased amount of their assistance.

The recent race troubles should not discourage us
or our friends. In fact, we should be encouraged,
for during these troubles the better element of the
race has been severely tried and they have stood the
test. Everywhere their advice has been for modera-
tion, patience, and forbearance. It is true, we are
troubled on every side, yet not distressed; we are perplexed, but not in despair; persecuted, but not forsaken; cast down, but not destroyed. Our records will
show that we have been faithful over a few things,
may we not retain the faith and trust of friends?

CHAPTER 14.

THE GREATEST MENACE OF THE SOUTH.

In every age there are great and pressing problems to be solved,—problems whose solution will have seemingly, a far reaching and lasting effect upon the economic life of the country concerned. It was the case in this country from its very beginning and the same condition obtains today, although each section of the country has its own peculiar problems the true American citizen recognizes the fact that the success of one section in solving its problems will be beneficial to the entire nation.

Perhaps, no section of this country has been confronted with more difficult problems than the South. I therefore, wish to present what I consider to be the greatest menace of this section, not as a prophet foretelling future events,—but humbly expressing my views of the situation after careful study.

If you were to ask the average white man of the South today what is the greatest menace to this section, his answer, undoubtedly, would be, the Negro and Negro domination. At least this would be the answer of the politician. That he would take this view, is shown by the great amount of legislation that has been enacted, aiming either directly or indirectly to retard the Negro's progress. I do not believe that there has been one piece of legislation enacted in the South within the last thirty years for the express purpose of promoting the Negro's welfare. This does not mean, however, that the entire white South is against the Negro or that it means to oppose his advancement. There are thousands of white men and women throughout the length and breadth of the South, who are today, laboring almost incessantly for the advancement of the Negro. To these, we owe a great debt of gratitude, and to these should be given much credit for what has been accomplished. This class of white southerns are not, as a rule, politicians and it is seldom, if ever, they are elected to office. When we speak of the average southern white man then, we have particular reference to the great horde of office seekers and politicians that infest the entire south-land. It is this class that will tell you that Negro domination is the greatest menace to the South.

Now, Negro domination may be a menace to the South, but it is certainly not the greatest. Neither is the extermination of our forests to be greatly feared. There are organizations and societies on foot in all parts of the South for the conservation of our forests.

Southern citizenship is suffering much from child labor, but even this, although being a great danger to our future development and prosperity, cannot rightly be classed as our greatest menace. The one thing today, in which we stand in greatest danger, is the loss of the fertility of the soil. If we should lose this, as we are gradually doing, then all is lost. If we should save it, then all other things will be added. Our great need is the conservation and preservation of the soil.

The increased crops which we have in the South occasionally, are not due to improved methods of farming, but to increased acreage. Thousands of acres of new land are added each year and our increase in farm production is due to the strength of these fresh lands. There is not much more woodland to be taken in as new farm lands, for this source has been well nigh exhausted. We must then, within a few years, expect a gradual reduction in the farm production of the South. Already the old farm lands that have been in cultivation for the past fifty or fifty-five years are practically worn out. I have seen in my day where forty acres of land twenty or twenty-five years ago would produce from twenty to twenty-five bales of cotton each year, and from 800 to 1000 bushels of corn. Now, these forty acres will not produce more than eight or nine bales of cotton and hardly enough corn to feed two horses. In fact, one small family cannot obtain a decent support from the land which twenty years ago supported three families in abundance. This farm is not on the hillside, neither has it been worn away by erosion. It is situated in the lowlands, in the black prairie, and is considered the best farm on a large plantation. This condition obtains in all parts of the South today. This constant deterioration of land, this gradual reduction of crops year after year, if kept up for the next fifty years, will surely prove disastrous to the South.

Practically, all the land in the black belt of the South is cultivated by Negroes and the farm production has decreased so rapidly during the last ten or fifteen years that the average Negro farmer hardly makes sufficient to pay his rent and buy the few necessaries of life.

Of course, here and there where a tenant has been lucky enough to get hold of some new land, he makes a good crop, but after three or four years of cultivation, his crop begins to decrease and this decrease is kept up at a certain ratio as long as he keeps the land. Instead of improving, the tenant's condition becomes worse each year until he finds it impossible to support his family on the farm. Farm after farm is being abandoned or given up to the care of the old men and women. Already, most of these are too old and feeble to do effective work.

Now, the chief cause of these farms becoming less productive, is the failure on the part of the farmers to add something to the land after they have gathered their crops. They seem to think that the land contains an inexhaustible supply of plant food. Another cause of this deficiency of the soil is the failure of the farmer to rotate his crop. There are farms being cultivated in the South today where the same piece of land has been planted in cotton every year for forty or fifty years. Forty years ago, I am told by reliable authority, that this same land would yield from one bale to one and a half per acre. And today it will take from four to six acres to produce one bale.

Still another cause for the deterioration of the soil is erosion. There is practically no effort put forth on the tenant's part to prevent his farm from washing away. The hill-side and other rolling lands are not terraced and after being in use four or five years, practically all of these lands are washed away and as farm lands they are entirely abandoned. Not only are the hillside lands unprotected from the beating rains and flowing streams, but the bottom or lowlands are not properly drained, and the sand washed down from the hill, the chaff and raft from previous rains soon fill the ditches and creeks and almost any ordinary rain will cause an overflow of these streams.

Under these conditions an average crop is impossible even in the best of years. At present, the South does not produce one-half of the foodstuff that it consumes and if the present condition of things continue for the next fifty years, this section of the country will be on the verge of starvation and famines will be a frequent occurrence. Of course, Negro starvation will come first, but white man starvation will surely follow. I believe, therefore, that I am justified in saying that there is even more danger in Negro starvation than there is in Negro domination.

I have noticed in this country that the sins of the races are contagious. If the Negro in a community be lazy, indifferent, and careless about his farm, the white man in the community will soon fall into the same habit. On the other hand, if the white man is smart, industrious, energetic and persevering in his general makeup, the Negro will soon fall into line; so after all, whatever helps one race in the South will help the other and whatever degrades one race in the South, sooner or later will degrade the other. But you may reply to this assertion by saying that the Negro can go to the city and make an independent living for himself and family, but you forget that all real wealth must come from the soil and that the city cannot prosper unless the country is prosperous. When the country fails, the city feels the effect; when the country weeps, the city moans; when agriculture dies, all die. Such are the conditions which face us today. Now for the remedy.

It is worth while to remember that there are ten essential elements of plant food. If the supply of any one of the elements fails, the crop will fail. These ten elements are carbon and oxygen taken into the leaves of the plant from the air as carbon dioxide, hydrogen, a constituent of water absorbed through the plant roots; nitrogen, taken from the soil by all plants also secured from the air by legumes. The other elements are phosphorus, potassium, magnesium, calcium, iron and sulphur, all of which are secured from the soil. The soil nitrogen is contained in the organic matter or humus, and to maintain the supply of nitrogen, we should keep the soil well stored with organic matter, making liberal use of clover or other legumes which have power to secure nitrogen from the inexhaustible supply in the air.

It is interesting to note that one of the ablest chemists in this country, Prof. E. W. Clark of the U. S. Geological Survey, has said that an acre of ground seven inches deep contains sufficient iron to produce one hundred bushels of corn every year for 200,000 years, sufficient calcium to produce one hundred bushels of corn or one bale of cotton each year for 55,000 years, enough magnesium to produce such a crop 7,000 years, enough sulphur for 10,000 years and potassium for 2,600 years, but only enough phosporus for 130 years. The nitrogen resting upon the surface of an acre of ground is sufficient to produce one hundred bushels of corn or a bale of cotton for 700,000 years;

but only enough in the plowed soil to produce fifty such crops. In other words, there are enough of eight of the elements of plant food in the ordinary soil to produce 100 bushels of corn per acre or a bale of cotton per acre for each year for 2,600 years; but only enough of the other two, phosphorus and nitrogen, to produce such crops for forty or fifty years.

Let us grant that most of our farm lands in the South have been in cultivation for fifty or seventy-five years, and in many instances for one hundred years, it is readily seen that practically all of the phosphorus and nitrogen in the plowed soil have been exhausted. Is it any wonder then that we are having such poor crops? The wonder is that our crops have kept up so well. Unless a radical change is made in our mode of farming, we must expect less and less crops each year until we have no crops, or such little that we can hardly pay the rent.

To improve and again make fertile our soils, we must restore to them the phosphorus and nitrogen which have been used up in the seventy-five or more crops that we have gathered from them. This is a herculean task but this is what confronts us and I for one, believe we can accomplish it. By the proper rotation of crops, including oats, clover, cowpeas, as well as cotton and corn, and a liberal use of barn-yard manure and cotton seed fertilizer, all of the necessary elements of plant food can be restored to our worn out soil. But the proper use of these require much painstaken study.

The black as well as the white should give this matter serious consideration. The landlords and the tenants should co-operate in this great work. The merchants and bankers must lend their aid and influence, preachers and teachers should be pioneers in this movement to save our common country. Our agricultural colleges should imprint their courses of study in something more than their annual catalogues. They should be imprinted in the minds and hearts of their students, and especially those who are to do farm work. Thus far, but very little general good has been accomplished by these schools. The reason is that the farmers, those who till the soil, have not had access to these schools and those who attend are not the farming class, and do not take to farming as their life's work. The man who works the soil must be taught how to farm. We have in this state nine purely agricultural schools, each of which is a white institution. It is true that some agricultural training is given for Negroes at Normal, Montgomery and Tuskegee, but these are not purely agricultural schools and the great mass of Negro farmers cannot hope to attend them.

If the Negro is to remain the farming class in the Black Belt of the South, then he must be taught at least the rudiments of the modern methods of improved farming. He must have agricultural schools and must be encouraged to attend them. The loss of the fertility of the soil is the greatest menace of the South. How can we regain this lost fertility, is the greatest question of the hour.

CHAPTER 15.

The Negro Exodus.

The Negro has remained in the South almost as a solid mass since his emancipation. This, in itself shows that he loves the South, and if he is now migrating to the East, North and West by the hundreds and thousands, there must be a cause for it.

We should do our best to find out these causes and at least suggest the remedy, if we cannot accomplish it. The time has come for plain speaking on the part of us all. It will do us no good to try to hide the facts, because "truth crushed to earth will rise again."

In the first place, the Negro in this country is oppressed. This oppression is greatest where the Negro population is greatest. The Negro population happens to be greater in the South than in the North, therefore, he is more oppressed in the South than in the North.

Take the counties in our own state. Some are known as white counties and others as black counties. In the white counties the Negro is given better educational opportunities than in the black counties. I have in mind one Black Belt county where the white child is given fifteen dollars a year for his education and the Negro child thirty cents a year. See the late Dr. Booker T. Washington's article, "Is the Negro Hav-

ing a Fair Chance?'' Now these facts are generally
known throughout this State by both white and black.
And we all know that this is unjust. It is oppression.
This oppression shows itself in many other ways.
Take for example the railroads running through the
rural sections of the South. There are many flag stations where hundreds of our people get off and on
train. The railroads have at these little stops a platform about six feet square, only one coach stops at this
point; the Negro women, girls and boys are compelled
to get off and on the train sometimes in water and in
the ditches because there are no provisions made for
them otherwise.

Again, take the matter of the franchise. We all
agree that ignorant Negroes should not be entrusted
with this power, but we all feel that where a Negro
has been smart and industrious in getting an education and property and pays his taxes, he should be
represented. Taxation without representation is just
as unjust today as it was in 1776. It is just as unfair
for the Negro as it is to the white man, and we all,
both white and black, know this. We may shut our
eyes to this great truth, as sometimes we do, but it is
unjust just the same.

Take the matter of the courts. There is no justice
unless the Negro has a case against another Negro.
When he has a case against a white man you can tell
what the decision will be just as soon as you know the
nature of the case, unless some strong white man will
come to the Negro's rescue. This, too, is generally
known, and the Negro does not expect justice.

None of us have forgotten the recent campaign of

Mr. Underwood and Mr. Hobson for United States Senator from this State. Mr. Underwood's supporters attacked Mr. Hobson because he defended the Negro soldiers when he was Representative, and Mr. Hobson's supporters attacked Mr. Underwood because they said that he had a Negro secretary in Washington. Any politician who dares defend a Negro, however just the cause may be, is doomed to political death. This is another fact which we all know.

As yet, there has been no concerted actions on the part of the white people to stop mob violence. I know a few plantations, however, where the owners will not allow their Negroes to be arrested unless the officer first consults them, and these Negroes idolize these white men as gods, and so far not one of these Negroes has gone North. I repeat that there are out-croppings of these oppressions everywhere in this country, but they show themselves most where the Negroes are in largest numbers.

All of these sorrows the Negro has endured with patience and long suffering, and they may be all classed as the secondary cause of this great exodus.

The primary cause is economics. The storms and floods destroy crops in the Black Belt section. These people are hungry, they are naked, they have no corn and had no cotton; so they are without food and clothes. What else can they do but go away in search of work? There are a great many wealthy white men here and there throughout the Black Belt section. They have large plantations which need the ditches cleared and new ones made to properly drain their farms. They could have given much work to these destitute people; but what have they done? Nothing. They say that it is a pity for the Negro to go away in such large numbers, and so it is, but that will not stop them. They have it in their power to stop them by making the Negro's economic condition better here.

The South must do more than make cotton and corn; it must begin to manufacture some of the things that it uses. Why should we send our raw material to the North to be manufactured? Practically all the furniture we use comes from the North and they get the timber from us. The South must be both a manufacturing as well as a farming section, if it would hold its own with the other sections of this great country. The capitalists of the South must turn loose their money if this section would come into its own.

Thus far, the average white man of the South has been interested in the Negro from a selfish point of view. He must now become interested in him from a humanitarian point of view. He must be interested in his educational, moral and religious welfare. We know that we have many ignorant, vicious, and criminal Negroes, which are a disgrace to any people, but they are ignorant because they have not had a chance. Why I know one county in this State today with 10,000 Negro children of school age and only 4,000 of these are in school, according to the report of the Superintendent of Education. We cannot expect ignorant people to act like intelligent ones, and no amount of abuse will make them better.

We know that our race is weak and that the white race is strong. We know also that our race is sick and that the white race is well or whole. Now, how should the strong treat the weak? How should the whole treat the sick? Would a strong man say, here is a weak man with a heavy burden, therefore, I will put more upon him? Would a well man say, here is a sick man, therefore, I shall give him less medical treatment? Then why do you say, here is the ignorant Negro, therefore let us give him less educational opportunities than we give the white man? If the white man would be logical in this particular, he would say in the courts, because he is ignorant let us make his punishment less severe; because he is weak, let us protect him, because he is ignorant, let us give him greater educational opportunities. But this has not been done. There has not been one dollar increase in the Negro public school fund in the rural districts in twenty years; if anything, it is less today than it was twenty years ago.

Sometimes we hear it said that the white man of the South knows the Negro better than anybody else, but the average white man of the South only knows the ignorant, vicious and criminal class of Negroes better than anybody else. He knows little of the best class of Negroes. I am glad to say, however, that there are a few Southern white men who know the better class and know them intimately and are doing what they can to better the Negro's condition. I would to God that the number of these few could be increased a hundred fold.

We used to deride the North for giving the Negro a chance to spend a dollar while withholding from him the opportunity to make one. But in the Providence of God all this has been changed by the great war in

Europe, which has created a labor scarcity in the North, East and West, and the Negro is now being given a chance to make a dollar there as well as spend one. The white man of the North is due no special credit for this, the credit belongs to God. He is the Righteous Judge of all the earth and in the end He will do right.

We will hear many tales of the sufferings of these people who go from this section. Many will die and some will come back, but still some will never return. You remember the fate of the Pilgrims, and the early colonists who first came to this country. You also know the fate of the men in the world war; many must die that some be saved. It behooves us of the South who remain here, both white and black, to re-dedicate ourselves to unselfish service and try more and more each day of our lives to live up to the great principle laid down in the memorable Atlanta speech by the immortal Booker T. Washington when he said: "In all things that are purely social we can be as separate as the fingers, yet one as the hand in all things essential to mutual progress."

CHAPTER 16.

THE NEGRO AND THE PUBLIC SCHOOLS OF THE SOUTH.

Too much praise cannot be given to the General Education Board, Dr. Dillard and Mr. Rosenwald, and others for what they have done and are doing to improve Negro public schools of the South, for in the last analysis it is there where the great masses of Negro children must be educated.

We have in the South, as every one knows, a dual system of public schools, one for the whites and one for the Negroes. This accounts in part for our poor schools for both white and colored. Such a system is expensive and, of course, the Negro gets the worst of the bargain. This is not surprising to him; he expects it in all such cases. He has been taught to expect only a half loaf where others get a whole one, but in some cases he gets practically nothing from the State for education. For an instance, I know four or five Negro public schools in the Black Belt that get $37.00 for the school term of four months. It would be hard to figure out how a teacher can live in these days on $9.25 per month. But, as I have said, the agencies that I have mentioned above have done much and are doing more to improve these conditions.

They endeavor to work with or through the State and county officials wherever it can be done. This I

TEACHERS OF SNOW HILL INSTITUTE

think is perfectly right and proper because the State must in the end direct the education of its subjects. But where this cannot be done, I think provision should be made for the thousands who are now being neglected.

Ever since I succeeded in getting the late Miss Anna T. Jeanes of Philadelphia to give so largely towards the Negro public schools of the South, I have been thinking how this work could be carried on in harmony with the State and county officials. The General Education Board, Dr. Dillard and Mr. Rosenwald have gone a long way towards solving this problem.

At the present time every Southern State has a Superintendent of Education and a County Superintendent. These officers are elected by the people (white people, of course). Recently, however, there have been two other offices created, State Supervisor of Education for the Negro and County Supervisor. These officers are selected and not elected. I think the offices came about as a result of the efforts of the General Education Board and Dr. Dillard, and I think that the State Supervisors of Education are selected largely through them.

Thus far all of the State Supervisors for Negro schools have been white men, and they in turn have been given the power to select the County Supervisor for the Negro schools, all of which are colored.

These white men are not always able to get the most efficient persons for such work because I know of a few County Supervisors here and there who are not competent to do the work that has been intrusted to them.

Now as the Negro has nothing to say as to who should be his State or County Superintendent of Education, it seems that in the matter of his State and County Supervisors he should have a word. (I think it is right and proper that the great funds for Negro education should be spent through the State and county officials wherever it can be done.)

The State Superintendent ought to be given the power to select the most competent Negro educator to be State Supervisor of Negro Schools, and the County Superintendent ought to be given the same. Furthermore, as each State has a Negro Education Association which meets once a year, I think this Association should recommend to the State Superintendent of Education a number of persons from whom he may select the State Supervisor. In each county we have an organization, which is known as the County Teacher Institute. This organization could recommend two or more persons to the County Superintendent from whom he might select the County Supervisor.

I feel and think in this way because in order to really help the people one must go amongst them and know of their hardships, struggles, desires, sorrows, and their joys, must talk with them, eat and sleep with them and know their hearts. It would be asking too much of the Southern white man to do this.

We know that in order to save the world God gave His only begotten Son, Jesus Christ, who came to earth in the likeness of man, to save man. Perhaps He might have sent an Archangel or an Angel, but this work of redemption could only be done by His sending a person who was a man, just like the men He was to save, and so it is with all great work of reformation and evolution.

In order to help the people we must become like them. In Christ becoming like man is what we call the humiliation of the Incarnation, and in that lies the great secret of redemption and reformation.

Again, I feel that this is a day of democracy, and that the Negro should be given a voice in the government of his schools. If this democracy, of which we are hearing so much, is for the white man alone, then I think that the Negro should know it, and if it is for all people he should know that.

The white man owes it to the Negro to make this matter plain.

CHAPTER 17.

WHERE LIES THE NEGRO'S OPPORTUNITY?

The liberation and enfranchisement of four million of slaves in this country fifty years ago brought into the body politic a situation that has ever since been a bone of contention. Because of their ignorance, most of these people were without the slightest idea of the proper use, or the power, of the ballot, and but few could properly exercise this new and high prerogative.

As long as the federal troops remained in the South and supervised and controlled the elections, these newly-made citizens retained their rights, but when, during President Hayes' administration, the troops were withdrawn, the South immediately set to work to remedy this condition. Starting with Mississippi in 1890, state after state disfranchised the Negro. Other discriminating laws have been enacted setting apart "Jim Crow" apartments for the Negro on all public carriers, establishing "Jim Crow" schools, and, in fact, segregating the two races in all public places wherever it is possible.

This action on the part of the South brought forth a storm of criticism from the North. The North accused the South of treating the Negro unjustly and taking from him his constitutional rights. The South answered the North, not by claiming its policy towards the Negro to be right, but by accusing the North of hypocrisy; but both sections agree that the Negro should be made as useful as his capacities will permit, and that he should seek the place where this usefulness can be best secured.

This long and constant agitation has led thoughtful students of the race problem to ask the question:

Are the conditions in the South more conducive to the social efficiency of the Negro than those offered to him in the North? This is a vital question and a just answer to it will have a far-reaching and lasting effect upon the future welfare of the Negro race in this country. By social efficiency we mean that degree of development of the individual that will enable him to render the most effective service to himself, his family and to society. As has been defined, all will agree that social efficiency is the chief end of life.

In the North the Negro lives mostly in the large cities, while in the South he lives mostly in the rural or country districts. Both the North and the South will admit this fact; the opportunities offered in the North then must be largely the opportunities such as large cities can offer, those in the South must be largely such as country districts can offer.

But before further considering this question let us note for a moment the opportunities offered in the South and those offered in the North. It is true that, in the South, the Negro is disfranchised. It is also true that he suffers many other injustices in that section, but on the other hand he has a wide field of labor.

First of all he has almost an unlimited opportunity to farm. He is better adapted to farm work in that

section than either the native white man or the
foreigner. He stands the heat better and can do more
work under a burning Southern sun.

In railroad construction the Negro is preferred.
The coal of the South is dug by Negro labor, the iron
ore is picked from the bowels of the earth by his
brawny muscles. The Negro finds work at the foun-
dries, the great pipe furnaces, the rolling mills, car
factories and other industries in the mineral districts.
He is eagerly sought for the sawmills, the turpentine
orchard, and in fact for almost every industry of the
South.

Though the white man in the South is beginning to
enter the field of industry, he has not entered to the
extent that the Negro's place is, in the least, in jeop-
ardy. Such are the opportunities offered the Negro in
the South, though he is largely deprived of political
and social rights. These facts are admitted by both
the North and the South.

Now what are the opportunities offered him in the
North? First of all, the Negro is a free man in a
political sense. He has the same right to vote that
other citizens have and, too, he can vote according to
the dictates of his own conscience.

President Roosevelt in his speech at Tuskegee in
1905, said that the colored people had opportunities
for economic development in the South that are not
offered to them elsewhere.

In the large cities of the North, where the Negro
mostly lives, the chances for good health and the purchase of a home are not so good. The man with little
means, such as the Negro usually is, must live in either

filthy streets or back alleys, where the air is foul and the environments are permeated with disease germs. For the lack of fresh air, pure food and proper exercise, his children are mere weaklings instead of strong and robust boys and girls.

Dr. Robert B. Bean of Ann Arbor, in his essay on "The Training of the Negro" in *Century Magazine* of October, 1906, said that in the large cities the Negro is being forced by competition into the most degraded and least remunerative occupations; that such occupations make them helpless to combat the blight of squalor and disease which are inevitable in these cities, and therefore many of them are being destroyed by them.

Mr. Baker says:

"One of the questions I asked of Negroes whom I met both North and South was this:

" 'What is your chief cause of complaint?'

"In the South the first answer nearly always referred to the Jim Crow cars or the Jim Crow railroad stations; after that, the complaint was of political disfranchisement, the difficulty of getting justice in the courts, the lack of good school facilities, and in some localities, of the danger of actual physical violence.

"But in the North the first answer invariably referred to working conditions.

" 'The Negro isn't given a fair opportunity to get employment. He is discriminated against because he is colored.' "

These conditions instead of promoting the social efficiency of the Negro, tend to degrade and demoralize him. The argument that the deprivation of the

Negro's political and social rights in the South tends to crush his ambition, warp his aspirations and distort his judgment, is unsound, because his self-reliance, ambition and independence in the South can be traced partly to this very deprivation. By it he has been forced to establish his own schools, his own churches, educate his own children and train his own ministers. All of these make for self-reliance and independence and are therefore conducive to his social efficiency.

CHAPTER 18.

School Problems of a Tuskegee Graduate.

"Two distinct problems face the Tuskegee graduate who goes forth as a leader of his people: the problem of extending education to the masses of our people and the problem of so adjusting the people to their actual conditions that the two races will be able to live and work together in harmony and helpfulness.

It may as well be admitted at the outset that the public schools in the rural districts of the lower South are not working toward this end. The condition of the public schools for our people in the Black Belt section of this state is disheartening. As unreasonable as it may seem, it is a fact that as the Negro population increases, in this section, the appropriation for Negro schools decreases. In many places the schools have been abolished altogether.

From almost every nook and corner of the South there comes a cry that the Negro as a laborer is unsatisfactory. It is said that he is inefficient, unreliable, indolent, lazy, in short, that he is unfit to do the work the South wants done. Less than two decades ago it was just the opposite. Then, it was said that the Negro was unfit for everything else except work. How inconsistent! We admit that there is a labor problem in the South, but we deny that it is due wholly to the inefficiency of the Negro as a laborer. In the first place, the natural increase of the population of the South has not kept pace with the marvelous growth and development of her industries. This in itself would explain a scarcity of labor. Furthermore, it should be remembered that the most industrious, the most frugal, and the most thrifty Negroes of the South are rapidly changing from the wage hands, to contract hands, and the day laborers, to the renters of their own farms, while thousands of Negroes in different parts of the South are establishing independent business enterprises for themselves. The South cannot hire that class of Negroes from their work. This, again has a tendency to make labor scarce. Added to this is the fact that thousands of Negroes are moving into the cities. Some are going into other states seeking on the one hand better educational opportunities for their children, and on the other hand, protection from mobs and lynchers. This again has a depressing effect upon labor.

While these underlying causes seem sufficient to account for the present labor troubles of the South, we must admit that there are entirely too many Negroes, particularly among those who work as wage-hands, contract-hands, and day laborers, who are ignorant and superstitious, too many who are gamblers and drunkards. Naturally, their work is not satisfactory. But they are not wholly to blame since they have had neither adequate educational opportunities, nor the proper home training. If they lack character, it is largely because they lack training. This is, as I understand it, what the President means when he says that "ignorance is the most costly crop that any community can produce."

Graduates from Tuskegee, a few years ago, received from our illustrious Principal the injunction, "Go ye into all parts of the South and change these conditions."

I will now try to give an account of my stewardship. I hail from Snow Hill, which is located in the heart of the Black Belt of this State, in a section where the colored people outnumber the white seven to one, and in the center of a colored population of more than 200,000. When we started work there twenty-five years ago the people as a whole were poor, ignorant, superstitious and greatly in debt. They had no special love for industrial training and not much general love for any kind of education. The so-called public schools were then running three months in the year and paying the teachers nine and ten dollars per month. We started work in a dilapidated one-room log cabin with three students and fifty cents in money. There was no state appropriation, neither was any church or society responsible for one dollar of its expenses.

Today we have an institution of more than four hundred students and twenty-two teachers and officers. We have 1940 acres of land, twenty-four buildings, counting large and small, and fourteen industries in constant operation. Being in a farming section, however, we are putting more stress upon agriculture.

It is the aim of our institution to teach the beauty and dignity of all labor and inculcate a love for the soil and for agricultural life. In spite of the denial of political rights and of the poor educational opportunities, and many other unjust discriminations, the South, just now, is the best place in this country for the Negro, and especially the agricultural section. We might as well recognize this fact and teach our people to act accordingly.

Again, we aim to train leaders for the masses of our people; for this purpose we need young men and young women imbued with the spirit of sacrifice and service who will go into these rural sections and teach our people how to live, how not to die; teach them how to live economically, to pay their debts, to buy land, to build better homes, better schools, better churches, and above all, how to lead pure and upright lives and become useful and helpful citizens in the community in which they live. Finally, we aim to train a high class of domestic servants. There need be no fear or uneasiness for we have an abundance of material for each class. But the worth of an institution is not determined by the acquisition of houses and land, neither by the bare statement of its aims, but by its actual power to serve the practical, daily needs of the community in which it exists.

As a result of our twenty-five years' work at Snow Hill, we have about one thousand graduates and ex-students who have either finished the full or partial course at the institution and are now out in the world doing creditable work as teachers, farmers, mechanics, and domestic workers. Over fifty per cent of our students have bought homes since leaving school. Many have houses with five and six rooms. Wherever a Snow Hill student teaches the school term is lengthened and the people are encouraged to buy land, build better homes, better school-houses and better churches.

The people have not only been helped by our students and graduates, but they have been helped directly through our Negro conference and Black Belt Improvement Society.

Twenty-five years ago the people in the neighborhood of the school did not own more than ten acres of land, while today they own more than twenty thousand acres. Twenty-five years ago the one-room log cabin was the rule, today it is the exception. Twenty-five years ago the majority of the farmers were in heavy debt and mortgaged their crops, today many of the farmers now have bank accounts, while a few years ago they did not know what a bank account was. Throughout the community they are building better homes, better churches, better school-houses, and the relation between the races is cordial.

Just a word about our Black Belt Improvement Society. This organization has ten degrees of membership and any one of good moral standing desiring to better his condition, can become a member of the first degree. A member of the second degree, however, must own a little property, at least three chickens, and a pig. A member of the third degree must own a cow, of the fourth degree he must own an acre of land, a member of the fifth degree must have erected on that acre a house having at least three rooms, a member of the sixth degree must own twenty acres of land, of the seventh degree must own forty acres of land, and of the eighth degree must own sixty acres, etc., until they reach the tenth degree.

Then we have an annual fair at which prizes are given to those who have excelled in any of the agricultural products, or those who have had the best gardens, or who have kept the best house during the year. a special prize is given to the party who has bought the most land during the year. This society has several committees. It has a committee on education. This committee holds meetings in the various communities to arouse in the people an interest in education. It encourages them to build better school-houses, to extend the school term and it keeps their children in school. It is the duty of the committee on labor to gather together those of our race who still work as contract-hands, wage-hands, day-laborers, and domestic servants, and impress upon them the necessity of rendering the best service, tell them that the race is judged more by what they do than what we do, and how great their responsibility is.

The farming committee is always active, trying to create in the people a real love for agricultural life, trying to show them that the opportunities which the country offers us are superior to those offered in the cities. Other committees are the committee on good government, committee on business, and committee on good roads. The influence for good this society is exerting throughout the section can hardly be estimated. Such is the nature of the work we are doing at Snow Hill.''

CHAPTER 19.

BENEFITS WROUGHT BY HARDSHIPS.

The word "Offence" is a general and somewhat indefinite term. As defined by the various dictionaries, it means an attack, an assault, aggression, injustice, oppression, transgression of a law, misdemeanor, trespass, crime and persecution. In all of these definitions there is implied an act considered as disagreeable if not harmful to the recipient.

Of the various nations of the earth, those that are most powerful and that have accomplished most good are those which have endured and have survived the most offences. They have grown by reason of the obstacles which they have overcome. It is singular, yet it is true, that offences have never destroyed a nation. Those nations which have been destroyed have been destroyed not by attack from without, but by their own internal weakness.

Societies that are accomplishing the most good for the uplift of humanity today are those against whom the most offences have been committed. Take the Christian Church, the greatest of all societies. Who can enumerate the offences which have been committed against the church? Herod tried to behead it, but could not; Pilate tried to crucify it, but instead sanctified it; Paul persecuted it and it redeemed him; poor drunken

and debauched Nero poured forth the fury of his wrath
against it in every conceivable, wicked way. He delib-
erately set fire to the city of Rome and accused the
Christians of the deed. He gave feasts in his garden
and the bodies of the Christians were burned as torch-
es in the evenings. Their groans and agonies constituted the music for their dance and carousal. Other
Christians were fed to half-starved lions. But through
it all the church has become more powerful and more
glorious than before; while Nero's name will forever
be a stench to the nations of the earth. In this particular case the prophecy of Christ "That offences must
need be but woe unto the man by whom the offence
cometh" is fulfilled. As with the church, so with all
other societies and institutions that are doing good
in the community, they endure their offences.

The history of the growth and rise of the various
races will show that they, too, have had their bitter
as well as their sweet. In fact, they have fought for
every inch of territory which they now possess.

Let us consider some of the benefits which have been
derived from our hardships. That the enslavement of
my people was a serious offence there is no doubt. I
should be the last one to apologize for slavery; but,
after all, we brought more out of slavery than we carried into it. We went into it heathens, with no language, and no God; we came out American citizens,
speaking the proud Anglo-Saxon tongue, and serving
the God of all the earth.

Under the leadership of old Richard Allen and other
noted colored divines, the Negro church was set up
under a bush harbor, but today they own church prop-

erty in this country valued at more than $26,000,000. As a result of the educational offences committed against the Negro, today he has 35,000 Negro teachers and more than seventeen million dollars' worth of school property in this country. The Negro has been disfranchised, but he is more capable of the ballot today than ever before. Though the disfranchisement of the Negro has wrought great harm to our Democratic form of government, it has increased in the Negro the spirit of patience, self-reliance, self-sacrifice, and, in fact, it has enhanced in him all of those virtues which make for true manhood and womanhood.

In the business world there has been less offence committed against the Negro than in any other way. What little there has been was rather slight and it has been only in recent years that the Negro has begun to detect it, and establish business of his own. He has not so many stores as he has schools, nor so many shops as he has churches, yet the reports of the Negro National Business League, which recently met in Atlanta, will show that he is making rapid progress in the business world.

All great men as well as races and nations suffered their offences. Washington, Lincoln and Grant were great because they had to endure hardships. Robert Small, Frederick Douglas and Booker Washington are great because they were slaves.

The Negro of the South was emancipated 50 years ago without education, without money, without clothes, without food, without even a place to rest his head, and, in many instances, without a name. His greatest possession was ignorance. If, during slavery, he was taught many useful and helpful lessons, during slavery, also, he was denied the opportunity of exercising and developing the greatest requisite of independence, self-reliance. He was a new-born babe, as a ship in mid-ocean without a rudder. It was nothing more than natural for him at times to drift, at times to wander, and still at other times to steer in the wrong direction.

Consequently, he made many mistakes, some of them serious. He made mistakes in religion, mistakes in economics, and mistakes in politics, but to my mind his greatest mistake was made in the matter of education. Until the year '95 the masses of our people in the Black-Belt section of the South believed that the end of education was to free one from manual labor, especially from the labor of the farm. They furthermore believed that it was the end of education to take the people from the country to the cities and otherwise fit them for only three callings, namely, of teacher, of preacher, and of politician. This conception of education was entertained not only by the masses, but many of our schools and colleges encouraged the same view.

Just at this period, when the relation between the races seemed most strained, there loomed on the horizon the Booker Washington idea, ''That the kind of education most needed by our people was that which would dignify, beautify, and make attractive and desirable country life and at the same time fit our people for high and useful citizenship.'' Mr. Washington further contended that any education which did not manifest itself in the practical daily life of the people was not worthy of the name.

This idea of Mr. Washington was indeed timely, but, like all other great movements for reform, it was not accomplished without obstacles, but in the face of many dangers and difficulties. But the dawn of a new day is breaking and industrialism seems to be the spirit of the age. The very fact that the Negro was not allowed to attend the white man's school in the South gave the Negro a Tuskegee. The fact that no white educator was willing to bear the black man's burden gave him a Booker Washington. For similar reasons the Negro has been forced to build his own libraries, his own theatres, his own hotels, and to establish many other business enterprises.

Hardships, trials, persecution, and offences are a primary necessity in life. We ought not, therefore, complain of them; our trials have made us what we are.

This is pre-eminently a progressive age. The world no longer stands still. We are either going forward or backward, rising or falling; there is no such thing as standing still. Those phases of our human activities that are standing still are dying. This forward movement is not accomplished without obstacles, and what is true of politics and business is equally true of individuals. The greatest strength comes from overcoming—from resistance and struggle.

CHAPTER 20.

The Negro and the World War.

No book written in the year 1918 would be complete without a word about this awful conflagration which is now sweeping over the earth.

One sometimes thinks that the end is near and that the world is being destroyed.

We know that everything that has been invented to advance civilization is now being used to destroy it. Our one consolation is that however imperfect we may have been as a nation, we know that our cause is just and because of this we believe that in the end we will and must win. The right has always been more powerful than the wrong, even more powerful than might and it will prove true in this case.

I am being constantly asked by white men in both the North and South, "How does the Negro regard this war and what about his willingness to share in its responsibilities." I have only one answer for such questions: "The Negro now knows but one word 'Loyalty.' He is no alien, he owes no allegiance to any other country, there is no hyphen to his name, he is all American, he is willing to fight and die, that the world might be made safe for democracy." He only asks that he may share in this democracy.

Already there are practically 200,000 Negroes who

have been called to the colors and thousands of others are expected to be called. I hear of but few if any slackers among them, while thousands of slackers of other races are being rounded up by the police in various cities throughout the country.

The 200,000 Negro soldiers who are now at the front and in the camps have gone with as brave hearts as any American citizen. They say, "Silver and gold, have I but little, but I give my life to Uncle Sam, it is all that I can do."

The Negro is not only furnishing men to the National Army, but he is doing his part to support the boys at the front. He has bought Liberty Bonds to the fullest extent. Many of his business organizations, societies and lodges have bought large blocks of these bonds.

On Sunday morning, June 14th, Dr. Cortland L. Myers of Tremont Temple, Boston, in his sermon told of an incident of an old colored woman who had worked hard and saved up three hundred dollars in order that she might not at the end be buried in the paupers' field, but when she read that the United States wanted money, took all she had and carried it to the bank to the agent. When the agent gave her the Liberty Bond and told her that she would get four per cent on her money, she was utterly surprised and said, "Lord, Boss, I thought I was giving this money to Uncle Sam." This woman had only three hundred dollars, but she gave all.

You remember what Christ said about those who were contributing to a great cause on one occasion. Many made large gifts, but one poor woman came up and gave a penny which was all she had. Christ on commenting on this to his Disciples said that she had given more than all, because she had given all she had. Many incidents of this kind may be cited as proof of the Negroes' loyalty in this struggle.

Not only in the Liberty Loan drive, but in the Red Cross and War Savings Stamp drives, the Negro is doing his part. There are Negro agents all over the South who are educating our people up to what the Government at Washington wants. Such schools as Snow Hill, Laurinburg, Denmark, Utica, Okalona and Calhoun and many others are serving as bureaus of information for this war work among the Negroes.

Nor is this all. The Negro is doing his part in the various industries of the country. I have heard of many strikes and walk-outs since we entered the war, but not once have a group of Negroes struck. In some places where a few are working with the unions, the unions have forced them out at the risk of their lives, but where he is free, nowhere in this country has the Negro struck during the war.

He is doing his bit on the farm. Everywhere the Negro farmers, man, woman and child, believe that they can help win the war by making a good crop and they are at work on the farm trying to do this, so you see that the Negro in every way is in the war to a finish.

These are answers to questions asked me by the white man both North and South as to the attitude of the Negro toward this world's war.

But on the other hand the Negro soldiers and civilians are not asleep and they too are asking such questions as these :—

"Are we to share in the democracy for which we are
     giving our lives?
When the world is made safe for democracy, will the
     entire country be made safe for it?
Will my father, mother, sister and brother be allowed
     to share in this democracy?
Will lynchings and burnings at the stake cease?
Will the white man who makes the laws allow these
     laws to take their course?
Will they allow us or give us a fair trial before their
     courts, which have only white men as jurors?
Will they cease taxing us without representation?
Will they give us an equal part of the money spent for
     education? (In many places in the Black Belt the
     Negro child receives thirty cents a year for edu-
     cation, while the white child receives fifteen dol-
     lars.) Will the Negro be given any work that he
     is capable of doing and not be denied it on account
     of his color?
Will it be possible for a Negro travelling from Ala-
     bama to California or Massachusetts, to find a
     place to sleep at night?
Will the baggage masters and the conductors of the
     South ever treat the Negro passengers with cour-
     tesy and respect and finally will the white man in
     the South after making the laws for the qualifica-
     tions of voters, allow a Negro to vote if he meas-
     ures up to these qualifications?

     The Negro does not care what these qualifications
may be. He only wants a fair chance in case he meas-
ures up to them.

The Negro only seeks equal rights and justice before all the courts of the land. He expects this because of his teachings. He was brought to this country against his will, even against his protest. He has been given the white man's language, his history, his literature, his Bible and even his God. His aspirations, inspirations and desires have been brought about as a result of these and if they are wrong, the white man is to blame. The Negro has been taught to believe that God is no respecter of persons and therefore his subjects should not be. He thought that if he did what other men did he would obtain the same results.

Now evidently the Negro is a man. He loves as other men do, he lives as others do, he dies as others die, he has joy and sorrow as others do, even hates as others do, laughs and cries as others. He must therefore, be a man as man is the only being which possesses these faculties. Then he asks for a man's chance and the world will never be right until this is given him. The world will never be safe for democracy until all the races of the earth are allowed to share in it.

In answer to all of the foreging questions asked me by both the white and black, I have said that things will be better for the Negro after the war. I have said that it was impossible for the world to be made safe for democracy unless every county in the South is made safe for it.

I have gone as far as to cite a recent occurrence in Camden, Wilcox County, Alabama, where more than one hundred and forty Negroes were sent to the cantonments and I was asked to be one of the speakers on the occasion. The white people there gave the Negroes a great banquet and in my remarks after thanking them for their hospitality, I said "That it would be foolish and cowardly on my part to stand here in your presence and say that as a race we have no grievances, for we have them, but this is no time to air them. When the house is on fire it is no time for family quarrels, but the thing to do is to put the fire out and then we can adjust the quarrels after.

"Today our National house is on fire and it is the duty of every man, both white and black, rich and poor, great and small, to rise in his might and put the fire out and when the fire is out, we will see you about these grievances."

I went a step further and told that "already the war had brought some good results as this was the most democratic day that this little city had ever seen. Before the war, two expressions were commonly used by the white man and the Negro. The Negro's expression was this:—"I haven't any country," and the white man's expression was:—"This is a white man's country." Now both of these classes are saying, "This is our country." I further said that "we should win this war, because democracy was right and autocracy is wrong, and if we lose, and God forbid that we should, the fault will not be in democracy, but it will be due to the fact that we are not practicing what we preach."

At the close of my remarks many of the white citizens, including the judge, the sheriff, lawyers and other prominent men came forward and congratulated me on what I had said and some said that the white people of Camden needed more of such plain talk. I took these signs to mean that better things were coming for the Negro of the South after the war, but I must admit that when I read in the evening papers of June 27th that Senator John Sharp Williams of Mississippi had practically defeated the bill for women suffrage, because he said that he favored the vote for white women only and that the bill in its present form would not be allowed in his state—I must confess that this action almost took away all of my hopes especially after there was no one to rise and rebut his argument. There was no one in the United States Senate to speak for democracy for all the people. Now I think that just such spirit as this exhibited by that great Senator from Mississippi is at the foundation of this world's war and until that spirit is crushed, I fear that this war will continue. For of a truth, "God is no respecter of persons."

Now I have given my answers to both the Negro and the white man. What is the answer of the white man?

Are we fighting for democracy for all the people, or are we fighting for democracy for the white man only?

This question has never been answered by the white man, but it must be answered after this great war.

APPENDIX

"Two decades ago, twenty members constituting the class of '93, received their commission from the illustrious Principal of this great institution on yonder hill, to go ye into all parts of the South and teach and preach Tuskegee's gospel. This gospel was then as it is now, a gospel of service. Now after the lapse of twenty years we have assembled here to review the efforts of past years. Although twenty years are not long enough in which to record the life's work of a class, it is sufficiently long to indicate the direction in which this work is tending.

"So we come today, not so much to tell what we have accomplished as to tell what we are doing to renew our allegiance to our Alma Mater, and to assure its Principal and members of the Faculty that our motto, "Deeds Not Words," is still our guiding star. Four of our number have passed to the great beyond. We must therefore wait a later and greater day to hear their record read or told. Of the remaining sixteen, we have lost all communication with two, and it would be mere speculation for us to say what these two are doing. We can only hope, and do most fervently pray, that wherever they are they have with them the deep and abiding spirit of Tuskegee, and this we believe they have. This leaves then only fourteen live, vigorous and active members with which we are concerned. All of these, except one, have been engaged more or less in teaching. They are located as follows:

"Two in Normal School at Snow Hill, Alabama; one at the head of a large Industrial School at Topeka, Kansas; three in Birmingham, Alabama; one teaching in Miles Memorial College; one in Government Service; one doing settlement work; two are in Asheville, N. C., where they are engaged in teaching and doing settlement work respectively; another teaching in Dothan, Alabama; two in Montgomery, one of these teaching and the other doing settlement work; one in Selma, Alabama, farming and doing extension work; one at the head of a prosperous Industrial School at China, Alabama, and one teaching in Georgia. All have been remarkably successful and they have touched and made better the lives of more than five thousand souls. While losing their lives for others, they have saved their own somewhat, materially.

"Having been out on the tempestuous sea of life for twenty years amidst both storms and calms, it may not be out of place for us to speak a word of warning or make a few suggestions to those who are to set sail today, and to those who hope to go to sea at a later date. This, then, is our message. First of all, it is necessary for you to know where the work of the world is to be done.

"On one occasion during Christ's sojourn on earth, He took a few of His disciples with Him upon the mountain and there transfigured Himself. He clothed

Himself in heavenly beauty and splendor; He arrayed Himself in His Godlike power. These men were so overjoyed at this manifestation of His glory and power, that old Peter, impulsive as he was, spoke out and said: 'Lord, it is good for us to be here, if it be Thy will, let us build here three tabernacles, one for Thee, one for Moses, and one for Elias.' The place was so glorious that they wanted to abide there. But at the same time the multitude was waiting at the foot of the mountain, hungering and desiring to be fed; naked and desiring to be clothed; sick, and desiring to be healed. The work of Jesus Christ and His disciples was not on the transfigured mountain, but at the foot among the masses. So as they came down from the mountain, there met Him a man whose son was a lunatic, desiring that the Master might heal him.

"So on occasions like this when Dr. Washington takes us upon the mountain and reveals to us Tuskegee. in all of her beauty and splendor, we are likely, in such a state of ecstasy, to cry out saying, Principal Washington, it is good for us to be here, and let us build three tabernacles; one for thee, one for Armstrong, and one for Douglas. But my friends, we cannot abide here. We must go down to the foot of the mountain among the masses. We must go out into the rural districts for there it is that the people are a hungry and thirsty crowd, and there it is that the harvest is great, but the laborers are few, and there it is the work of the world must be done.

"Another suggestion is, that as you go out to work, you will find that for the most part Negro society is built upon a false basis. Instead of being built upon the sound basis of merit and character, it is built upon display; instead of being built upon substance, it is built upon shadow.

"We need young men and women who have confidence in themselves; confidence in the race, and abiding faith in God. We need young men and women who are more interested in the opportunity to make a dollar than in the privilege to spend one. We need young men and women who are imbued with the spirit of sacrifice and service, whose mission is, 'Not to be ministered unto, but to minister.' We need young men and women with a purpose.

"To illustrate what we mean by a purpose, we take the action of Grant during the late Civil War. When Winfield Scott and McClellan had practically failed with the army of the Potomac and things were looking very dark for the Union forces, Lieutenant U. S. Grant was placed in command of all the Union forces. From the date of his command, his purpose was: 'On to Richmond.' Day after day his command was: 'On to Richmond.' When they had rivers to ford and mountains to climb, his command was: 'On to Richmond.' At times thousands were laid low by the ravage of disease, but his command was: 'On to Richmond.' When the cannon of his enemy roared like thunder and bullets like lightning struck his men down by the tens of thousands, his command was: 'On to Richmond.' He received letters and telegrams by the thousands saying: 'My God, General, are you going to kill all of our husbands, all of our sons, our brothers? Are you going to make all of the North a land of widows and orphans?' His reply was: 'On to Richmond.'

When rivers of blood were before him, flames of fire swept over his forces, his command was: 'On to Richmond.' And the command never ceased until Lee surrendered his sword to Grant at Appomattox Court House. We repeat, that for the work that lies before us, we need young men and women with a purpose.

"A third warning is, that we must not mistake the aim and end of education. You will find somewhere in the Bible a sentence like this: 'And the word was made flesh and it dwelled among us.' The word had been spoken by Abraham; Moses thundered it from Mt. Sinai's rugged brow; Ezekiel preached it; David sang it; Solomon proclaimed it; Jeremiah prophesied it; Elijah saw it in the whirlwind; Moses saw it in the burning bush, and Isaiah saw it and in amazement cried: 'Who is this that cometh from Edom with dyed garments from Bazroh? this that is glorious in his apparel, traveling in the greatness of His strength?' But my friends, none of this would do. Speaking the word would not atone; hearing it would not redeem; and seeing it would not save. The word had to be made flesh and blood in the person of Jesus Christ, the Son of God, and then come down on earth and live, move, and dwell among us.

"As with the word, so with education. You have been here a number of years trying to obtain it. You have heard education from your teachers; you have heard it in the class-rooms; you have heard it from the platform; you have heard it in the Sunday-School; you have gleaned it from your text-books; you have sung it; you have prayed it; you have spoken it; you have walked it; you have assumed it. But none of these will suffice. Education, in order to be real, must be applied; in order to be effective, it must be digested and assimiliated. It must become a part of your flesh and blood; it must transform you into a new creature and then go out and move, live and dwell among us.

"And now a final word for the class of '93. What of its loyalty to Tuskegee, our Alma Mater? It is true that at times our purposes and aims have been misunderstood and misconstructed; at times your attitude towards us has been misinterpreted, but not once have we doubted your love. We hope that you have never mistrusted ours.

"It is true that at times we are troubled on every side, yet not distressed; we are perplexed, but not in dispair; persecuted, but not forsaken; cast down, but not destroyed. Through all of this, our love and loyalty to dear old Tuskegee has never wavered, and now as a token of this love and loyalty, I hand to Dr. Washington as a Memorial Scholarship for the class of '93, a check for one thousand dollars."

I think that this act pleased Dr. Washington more than anything that had ever been done by the class of '93. We all were proud of this because we wanted Dr. Washington to see that we had not forgotten what he had done for us. We wanted to do this during his lifetime, and this we succeeded in doing.

An address before the Alabama State Teachers' Association, held in Montgomery, Ala., the subject being:

"School Building Under Difficulties."

"There is no work pertaining to the welfare of our race that is of more importance than that of the teacher, and no class of people has a harder task to perform than the earnest and conscientious Negro teacher of today.

"The problems that come before the large educational associations of this and other countries, are problems dealing largely with the child, such as the treatment of backward children, treating of abnormal children, care of the blind, of the deaf, special treatment for incorrigibles, the feeble minded, and many other kinds of mental and physical defectives.

"Other problems that demand the attention of such meetings, are problems dealing with the teacher, his preparation and qualification for the various grades of our schools, for instance, preparation of the teacher for the elementary school, for the secondary school, and for colleges and universities. These associations also give much time to such subjects as The Relation of Education to Real Life; The Defects of our Present School System; and how these defects may be remedied. In other words, how can the school better fit the student to take his place in the social and economic life of today? I repeat, these are the problems which largely consume the time of these educational meetings. They are vital and far-reaching, and demand the closest attention of our wisest and best educators. They are not racial; not sectional; not even national, but are universal in their scope and teachers in all parts of the world must contend with them.

"The average Negro teacher of the South today must assume his share of the burden of these problems along with other teachers, whether he wills it or not. In addition to this he has to deal with the serious problem of his bread and butter. This makes the burden of the Negro teacher of a two-fold nature, and in this respect he is at a disadvantage of the average American teacher. He has not as yet been able to live up to the Biblical injunction, 'Take no thought for your life, what ye shall eat, or what ye shall drink, nor yet for your body, what ye shall put on.' No teacher can do his best so long as there is doubt and uncertainty about his daily bread.

"The Negro student who finishes at one of our higher institutions of learning today, and goes forth to teach, does not find everything to his liking. He soon learns that there has been no voice before him crying in the wilderness saying: 'Prepare ye the way of the teacher, make straight in the desert a highway for our educator.' He learns here for the first time that in addition to the ordinary educational problems, it is for him to exalt every valley, make low every hill and mountain, make the crooked straight, and the rough places plain. He finds no way prepared, he must make one; he finds no school-house ready, he must build one; he finds no people anxiously awaiting him, he must persuade them. In many cases the Negro teacher who is imbued with the spirit of sacrifice and service can truly say as did the Master, 'The foxes have holes and the birds of the air have nests, but the teacher who would redeem a poverty stricken and ignorant people, has not where to lay his head.'

"The purpose of the Snow Hill Institute is to prepare young men and young women to go into communities where they propose to work and influence the people to stop living in rented one-room log cabins, buy land, and build dwelling houses having at least four rooms, and thus improve the home life of the people. Second, to influence the people to build better school-houses and lengthen the school terms and thus by arousing educational interest, assist in bringing about the needed reform that is so essential to economic and upright living; and finally to promote good character building. To some extent the purpose is being realized, for more than one thousand different students who have been more or less benefited by having spent a year or more under its guidance, are leading sober and useful lives. Two hundred fifteen have either been granted certificates or diplomas, and are engaged as follows: Fifty are teachers, twenty-five are housekeepers, three of the teachers have founded schools of their own, one at Laurinburg, N. C., one at West Butler, Alabama, and one at Richmond, Alabama.

"Though the majority of the ex-students are located in the Black Belt of Alabama and are engaged principally in farming, a large number of them are found in the following states: Mississippi, Louisiana, Georgia, Florida, and the Carolinas."

APPENDIX

"THE SIGNS OF TIMES"

It was customary in ancient times for nations to build walls around their cities to protect them from the enemy. War was the rule, and peace the exception. Nations therefore spent most of their time in preparing for war, as they believed that their advancement depended largely upon their conquest. Watchmen would be placed here and there on the walls to keep a sharp look-out for the enemy and when detected, would warn the inhabitants of his approach. As a result of these warlike times and military activities, some of the world's greatest generals were produced during that period.

Undoubtedly, conditions here mentioned, existed because of the poor methods of transportation and communication that were uncertain during that day, for since the advent of the steam-engine, telegraph, telephone, the automobile, and other means of rapid transit, national lines of demarcation have been becoming less distinct. As nations communed with nations and understood each other better, they found less causes for differences and less need of watchmen on the walls. We cannot help but believe that with a better knowledge of each race by the other and on the part of each a better understanding of the great and common end of life, which is to serve and uplift, that racial strife and conflict will cease and ere long this old world will become the kingdom of our God.

But these are not ancient times and things that were are not now. The cities of the plain are no longer separated, for the walls have been demolished and instead of the watchmen we have the teacher, the preacher and the politician to tell us the signs of the times.

This is, pre-eminently, a progressive age; an age of going forth; an age in which things move. With the new and varied inventions of the 19th and 20th Centuries, old customs and conditions are rapidly passing away and those nations, races, and individuals who cannot adjust themselves to these new conditions must be left behind. Just now grave and serious problems confront the American People and this, in itself, is a proof of our going forth. We must not deprecate them, we must not shirk them, they are ours, we must face them manfully, must shoulder them and stand up and walk. These problems are the mothers of progress and instead of trying to turn from them or to dodge them, we should rejoice because we live at a time when we can help in the solution of such complex problems, whose results will have such far reaching and lasting effect upon the social and economic life of the American People.

This country is one and inseparable and whatever is beneficial to the white man is beneficial to the black man also. The negro cannot hope at the present to play a very important part in the solution of great questions. At our best the part we must play can only be secondary. First, because our business operations have not brought us into intimate relation to these questions and we do not fully comprehend their meaning. Second, we can do but little because these questions are political in their nature and must be settled by the ballot. The Negro in this section has been disfranchised and therefore he cannot play at that game. Our being thus handicapped and prohibited from assisting in the solution of these great problems, is no reason why we should say there is nothing we can do.

"If you cannot cross the ocean
And the heathen lands explore
You can find the heathen nearer;
You can help them at your door.

There are some problems, however, that are within our reach, upon the solution of which depends our future welfare in this country. They are, inefficiency, vagrancy, and crime. For a long time we have been hearing of the inefficiency of the Negro teacher, the inefficiency of the Negro preacher, but all the while it was said that he was a good worker; that he was only fitted to do manual labor. The cry has gone out and is rapidly spreading to the effect that the Negro is worthless; that there is inefficiency in the pulpit, inefficiency in the school-room, and now inefficiency on the farm. Inefficiency everywhere. Our race has lost many places of trust and honor because of this cry. I know personal cases where Negro men have been replaced by white men because, they say, the black men were inefficient. This is as much true in New York as it is in Alabama. As the supply of efficient men increases, the demand for inefficient men will decrease and sooner or later there will be no room for the inefficient man. He will be idle, cannot get any work to do. He will be added to the vagrant class. Already this class is too large among us; strong able-bodied men walking about with no home and nothing to do. This is a dangerous class. Of course, unless the vagrant gets some work to do he will starve or have to leave the country; but this man does not do either. He becomes a parasite and lives of the honest toil of others. Sometimes he lives out of the white man's kitchen, because his sweetheart is the cook; sometimes because his old mother is a wash woman, and sometimes because his sister is a nurse. This is the class, my white friends, that gives you trouble, this is the class that gives us trouble, this is the class that will give trouble to any community and we are as anxious as you are to rid ourselves of this body of death.

Now the best class of Negroes and the best class of white people are agreed as to the fact that this dangerous class must be gotten rid of, but they differ as to methods. The Negro believes mostly in the preventive method, the white man mostly in the cure method. The Negro says a good school in every community will prevent, the white man says a good jail in every county will cure. The Negro says teach the law, the white man says enforce the law. The Negro cries for a state reformatory for the boys and girls of his race, the white man cries for the penitentiary for them. Now, this is not a very great difference after all and we should get together by each asking for the best schools to prevent these evils and then when the evils are committed, asking for the strictest law for their punishment. As for my part, it is not a question in my mind as to the cause of this increasing class among my people. It is plain to me that ignorance is the cause of inefficiency, inefficiency the cause of vagrancy, and vagrancy the cause of crime. We must, therefore, seek the remedy in the removal of the cause. If ignorance be the mother of inefficiency, inefficiency the mother of vagrancy, and vagrancy the mother of crime, it is plain that the removal of ignorance will stop the others. This can only be done by education and civic righteousness.

I wish here to emphasize the fact that education is the source of all we have and the spring of all our future joys. Our religion, our morality, and that which is highest and best in our social and civic life, all come from education. Therefore, it is the primary factor in the elevation of all races.

Our education should be of a threefold nature, viz.: Literary, Industrial and Religious. No limit should be placed upon the Negro's literary qualification. A race so largely segregated as ours, needs its own teachers, preachers, lawyers. doctors, pharmacists, and other professional and business men, and therefore they should be given the highest and best education that is obtainable. If our preachers and teachers are inefficient, it is because they are improperly educated. If the churches are growing cold and dying and the schools accomplishing but very little good, it is because religion is not being made practical and education not being made to apply to our every day life. Such an end can only be accomplished through well and systematically trained teachers and preachers. Better teachers and better preachers will go a long way towards the alleviation of our ills. If we would secure the kind of education here referred to, we must be willing to pay for it; we must make a sacrifice, we must care less about forms and fashions and more about the higher things of life. We must see less evils in the dollar and more good.

We must not only have a good education, but we must have good industrial training. This is a scientific as well as a literary age. A scientific age is always an age of inventions and with new inventions comes the demand for men qualified to manage large interests and complicated machinery. This demand can only be supplied by industrially trained men and women. This must be done in our industrial schools. Our hands should be as truly trained to work as our minds to think, and any education that teaches otherwise, is not worthy of the name.

I know that in some sections my people are prejudiced towards industrial schools, but this is foolish in the extreme. If we are to hold our own in this country, it must be by our ability to do work and to do it in the most acceptable manner. We are in a farming section and I believe that we should therefore strive to be the best farmers in the world. Let us make a specialty of all the trades that are related in anyway to agriculture; endeavor to become the best stock raisers, the best truck gardeners, the best cooks, the best wash women, the best housekeepers, the best dress makers, the best blacksmiths, and in fact, the best in all that pertains to country life.

Let us get hold of the lands we cultivate as far as possible and build better homes and keep our homes clean. But you say that we do not need industrial training. Let us see. Many years ago Henry Clay, in order to encourage home industry, introduced a bill in the Kentucky Legislature to the effect that the people of that state should use nothing save what could be produced in the state. Suppose today the white man of this country should say that the Negro must use only the things which he could make, what would be his condition? Could we cook with proper utensils? Could we eat with knives and forks? Could we dress as we do now? Practically everything we wear or use was made by the white man and were he to institute such actions we would be helpless to provide for ourselves.

In our quest for knowledge, we must not overlook the education of the heart. Our religion should be made practical. It must be real and not visionary. No other will suffice. Our religion must consist more in deeds and less in words.

EPILOGUE

Consuela Lee

The long drive home to Snow Hill, Alabama, in April 1979 had finally come to an end as the road turned into the campus of Snow Hill Institute. I stopped the car in the middle of the campus and carefully surveyed the grounds. The academic halls, dormitories, and trade buildings erected under the Edwards administration had long since been destroyed by fire. The few buildings remaining were obviously abandoned, abused, and badly in need of repair. The rolling lawns were overgrown with high weeds.

Snow Hill Institute was closed in 1973 by a court-ordered desegregation edict. In fact, the closing was an act of mercy, for the school had lost its academic prestige, its purpose, and its mission and was in desperate need of a new beginning.

As I resumed my drive up the hill past the Edwards House to the home of my mother, Alberta Grace Edwards Lee, my resolve to work toward rebuilding this once-proud citadel of learning became a passionate commitment.

To prepare for restoring the historic school, I thought it essential to gain insight into the man who founded and built Snow Hill Institute, William James Edwards. Alberta, second oldest of the Edwards children, had placed the Edwards Papers[1] in her home after the death of my grandmother, Susie, in 1973. I asked my mother for permission to borrow the papers, which were stored in a bedroom chest of drawers in an old letter file box. I remembered seeing the old box many times, but looked upon it now in a different light, in a more meaningful way. I lifted it from the drawer and carefully opened its latch. Clipped to the first of the yellowed pages was a note handwritten by my brother, William James Edwards (Bill) Lee III. It was a simple and fitting epitaph to our maternal grandfather: "PAPA WAS A GREAT MAN."

* * * * *

William James Edwards married Susanna Verdell Johnson (who preferred being called "Susie") in 1900. Six children were born to this union—Marina Blanche Edwards Stone, Alberta Grace Edwards Lee, Geneva Belle Edwards Brown, William James Edwards, Jr., Wendell Howell Edwards, and Hope Christabelle Edwards MacMillan.

The children of the founder/principal of Snow Hill Institute, who lived in the large white house overlooking the campus, were brought up under the heavy rule of their father's iron hand. "Papa" (as children and grandchildren called him) was a strict disciplinarian who did not spare the rod. Even though Mrs. Edwards ("Mama") had the luxury of female students helping her with housework in exchange for tuition and board, certain chores were demanded of the children, including working in the fields.

The Edwards children were students at Snow Hill Institute during its glorious, golden years. Papa was well known and highly respected throughout the Deep South as well as in parts of the Northeast. Alberta speaks of the royal treatment afforded the Edwards family whenever they visited Tuskegee Institute during Dr. Booker T. Washington's presidency. All the children chose teaching careers and all played musical instruments, reaching varying degrees of accomplishment. Alberta was exceptionally talented and became a brilliant pianist, thanks to her father's policy of hiring excellently trained musicians as well as affording her the opportunity to spend summers studying at the New England Conservatory in Boston and at Fisk University in Nashville.

*   *   *   *   *

Growing up in the thirties and forties in Snow Hill, I remember Papa as an introspective, gentle, intellectual man who was politically astute. He subscribed to the *New York Herald Tribune* and was a staunch Republican who abhorred the Democrats for harboring rabid racists. In one of his speeches he castigated Franklin D. Roosevelt and his New Deal: "We don't need handouts, we need justice!" He enjoyed sitting on his porch swing smoking a pipe, feet up, his body fitting in the seat perfectly. Oftentimes, a friend from the community would come to visit, engaging him in long conversation.

Ligon A. Wilson, principal of Snow Hill Institute from 1929 to 1948, would often invite Papa to speak at Vesper Service, a Sunday evening tradition inherited from Tuskegee Institute. Students and faculty were spellbound by the dramatic delivery of this splendid orator. His text was usually taken from the Bible, and occasionally he was emotionally overcome after finishing his sermon, wiping tears from his eyes as he resumed his seat on the stage.

Sometimes he had speaking engagements away from Snow Hill. At that time the Louisville & Nashville Railway provided roundtrip passenger service between Selma and Flomaton, Alabama. Snow Hill was one of the stops. In a letter dated April 23, 1947, Mama wrote to her son William ("Buddy") who lived in Dayton, Ohio: "Mr. Edwards has gone down to speak at Pat Carmichael's closing. He is happy when he gets an opportunity to speak."[2]

He was a biblical scholar, impeccable in his recitation of complete chapters and psalms. On special occasions I was privileged to eat downstairs in Mama's dining room along with other select grandchildren. After all were seated, Mama would call Papa (his room was at the top of the stairs to the right): "Mist' Edwards!" He would walk downstairs carefully with his cane hooked over his arm and take his seat at the head of the table. We were very quiet and respectful as we bowed our heads, Mama's hot, buttered rolls teasing our senses. "I will lift up mine eyes unto the hills,/ From whence cometh my help . . . ," Papa intoned reverently. We kept our heads down for the rendering of the entire biblical passage. He recited from memory, dramatically emphasizing certain words, speaking with deep emotion.

Papa was also a farmer, continuing to sow and harvest until he was physically unable to do so. One summer he hired five or six of us older grandchildren to chop in his cotton and corn fields. We were paid twenty-five cents per week, and he enjoyed lining us up in his bedroom (a rather sacred, rarely visited place for me that had the heavy and heady smell of tobacco and old wool suits) to dole out the payroll. This family business venture soon came to an end after the laborers were deemed incompetent.

*   *   *   *   *

"When Papa lost the school" was a phrase often heard in the Edwards family when I was a young person. It had a mysterious, rather intriguing ring and certain occurrences, when related, were pinpointed in terms of this momentous happening, as in: such-and-such took place *before* Papa lost the school or *after* Papa lost the school. *Why* Papa lost the school in his mid-fifties, generally considered to be the prime years of school administrators, was discussed out of earshot of the younger generation.

My mother admits it was a terrible time. She had married Arnold Wardsworth Lee and was living in Tallahassee, Florida. The academic year was 1926–27. Papa had recovered from, most probably, a severe nervous breakdown, only to be confronted with the realization that the school that he had founded, had made his life's work, had nurtured, and for which he had sacrificed had been wrested from him.

In anger and consternation he withdrew his daughter, Hope, from Snow Hill Institute. It was her senior year, and she was sent to Tallahassee to live with Alberta and Arnold and attend school there. Hope was the only one of the Edwards children who did not graduate from Snow Hill Institute.

*   *   *   *   *

William J. Edwards was a man of great courage, spiritual depth, intellect, and vision. He honored and glorified his people by sacrificing immeasurably to bring them out of the bleakness of dependence and destitution into the light of independence and land ownership, and by building a school that offered them education, skills, and cultural arts that allowed them to grow in mind and spirit.

NOTES

1. The Edwards Papers are a collection of sermons, speeches, business letters, political positions, and prophecies.
2. Patrick Carmichael (1886–1989), a relative of the Edwards family, graduated from Snow Hill and founded a school in Perdue Hill, Alabama.